DATE DUE

INDIRA GANDHI

A LERNER BIOGRAPHY

INDIRA GANDHI
Daughter of India

CAROL DOMMERMUTH-COSTA

Lerner Publications Company / Minneapolis

For young women everywhere
who know that strength and courage
are part of being a woman.

Lerner Publications Company
A division of Lerner Publishing Group
241 First Avenue North
Minneapolis, Minnesota 55401 U.S.A.

Website address: www.lernerbooks.com

Library of Congress Cataloging-in-Publication Data

Dommermuth-Costa, Carol.
    Indira Gandhi / Carol Dommermuth-Costa.
        p.   cm. — (A Lerner biography)
    Includes bibliographical references and index.
    ISBN 0–8225–4963–8 (lib. bdg. : alk. paper)
    1. Gandhi, Indira, 1917–1984—Juvenile literature. 2. Prime ministers—India—Biography—Juvenile literature. [1. Gandhi, Indira, 1917–1984. 2. Prime ministers. 3. Women—Biography. 4. India—Politics and government—20th century.] I. Title. II. Series.
    954.04'5'092—dc21   00-010435

Manufactured in the United States of America
1 2 3 4 5 6 – JR – 07 06 05 04 03 02

Contents

A very young Indira Gandhi poses for a family portrait with her mother, Kamala, and father, Jawaharlal Nehru.

 ONE

The New Soul of India

1917–1921

Indira woke up and looked at her surroundings. Accustomed as she was to a luxurious home, she could hardly believe where she was. Mud-colored walls and floors stared back at her, as if mocking her sense of beauty and grace. Her drab, brown clothes were dirty and stained. Even her food tasted dry and gritty. Everything was devoid of softness and color. She remembered the words of the writer Oscar Wilde: "Each day is like a year, a year whose days are long." Indira was in prison, and she expected to be here for seven years.

She had been arrested the night before while demonstrating for Indian independence. As a child, she had watched helplessly as her father, her grandfather, and even her mother had been arrested and taken away from her.

Indira knew that her actions and the resulting arrest were for the best—perhaps not for her—but for her beloved country, India. Her family, along with thousands of others, had worked tirelessly for many years to wrench their country from the clench of British rule. This price she had to pay was only a small one compared to those who had lost their lives in the fight for liberty.

India is a land of great variety and contrast. Geographically, the country includes the Himalaya—the world's highest mountain system—scorching desert, lush rain forests, and tropical lowlands. Most Indians are farmers who live in mud-and-straw dwellings in villages and work the surrounding fields, but a growing number of people are moving to cities. Kolkata (formerly Calcutta), Delhi, and Mumbai (formerly Bombay) are among the largest cities in the world. Modern high-rise apartment and office buildings stand in parts of the cities, but most people live in crowded slums. The Indian people belong to a wide variety of ethnic groups and speak hundreds of languages and dialects, but India's national language is Hindi. Food and clothing also vary throughout the country. Indians practice many different religions, but the majority are Hindus.

The caste system further divides the Indian social structure. Traditionally, Indians—especially Hindus—have been organized into social groups called castes, or *varnas*. A person's caste determines his or her social status and influences what occupation a person might hold. Ancient Hindu texts describe four main castes. The Brahmans (priests and scholars) were the highest group, followed by Kshatriyas (rulers and warriors), Vaishyas (merchants and professionals), and Shudras (artisans, laborers, and servants). Complicated rules govern contact between members of different castes. For example, when members of a caste eat cooked food, it must be prepared by a member of the same caste or a higher caste. About fifteen percent of the Indian population is outside the caste system. Known as the untouchables, this group has traditionally held the most undesirable jobs, and some upper-caste Indians think they will be polluted by touching members of this group. Under the Indian Constitution, the untouchables are supposed to have equal rights, but they remain an oppressed group, especially in villages.

The untouchables were traditionally the lowest caste in India and often faced mistreatment.

THE LANGUAGES OF INDIA

The Indian people speak more than one thousand languages and dialects—more than in any other place in the world. The two main language groups are Indo-Aryan and Dravidian.

Indo-Aryan is a branch of the Indo-European family of languages. Modern Indo-Aryan languages are based on Sanskrit, an ancient language. About three-fourths of the Indian population—mainly in north and central India—speak one or more of the main Indo-Aryan languages. These include Assamese, Bengali, Gujarati, Hindi, Kashmiri, Marathi, Oriya, Punjabi, and Sindhi.

The four main languages of the Dravidian family of languages are Kanada, Malayalam, Tamil, and Telugu. About one-fifth of the Indian population, located in the southern part of the country, speak these languages.

In northeastern India and along the border with Myanmar, many people speak Kuki, Manipuri, Naga, and other Sino-Tibetan languages. Other groups in the northeast speak Mundari and Santali, which belong to the Mon-Khmer or Austro-Asiatic family of languages.

More than two-fifths of the people speak one or more dialects of Hindi, the national language of India, and schoolchildren are required to study Hindi. English, however, is officially an associate national language spoken by most educated people across India. The nation's official business is conducted in English, and it is widely used in colleges and universities.

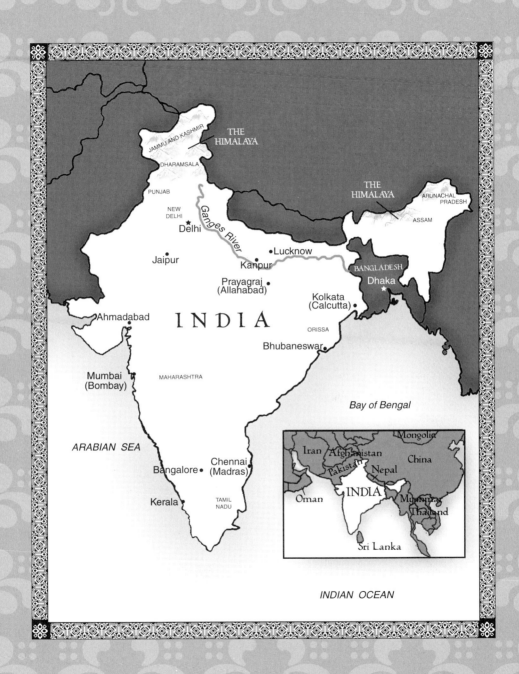

Politically, India has been a splintered country, with many small states ruled by various cultures over the centuries. From A.D. 500 until the mid-1800s, India had been taken over by various countries and cultures, including the Aryans from Russia, the Moguls from Siberia, the Muslims from Turkey, and the Portuguese. When Europeans, such as the Portuguese explorer Vasco da Gama, began to explore India, they returned home and told stories about a new land filled with strange people and exotic goods like spices and silks.

The central headquarters of the East India Company, circa 1655

In the 1600s, the East India Company, a British trading company, began trading with Indians for their products. Gradually, the company took over territories in India. British influence was felt everywhere, especially when the British began to impose their own laws and customs on the Indians.

In 1857 the Indians staged a rebellion against the British and the East India Company. The Indians fought valiantly, but the British squashed the mutiny. In 1858 the British government decided to govern India directly. British settlers established schools, churches, railroads, and a military force. The British decided that some Indian customs were barbaric and established laws forbidding such behavior.

At first, the Indians hesitantly accepted British rule. Many Indians believed they were not able to rule themselves as a united country. But gradually, many Indians began to feel uncomfortable being, in a sense, half Indian and half English. Their children went to British schools, they were subject to British laws, they were commanded by British troops. Many of their homes were decorated with British and European goods, but they were Indian, part of a culture that had thousands of years of history behind it. Many Indians began to question the presence of British culture and law in India.

In 1885 an Englishman named Allan Hume started the Indian National Congress, a political organization for those Indians who wanted an independent country. Indira's grandfather, Motilal Nehru, and her father, Jawaharlal Nehru, were members of the congress. Their philosophies differed, however. Motilal believed that the British had done a good job in ruling India. He believed that, in time, Britain would hand over the reins of self-rule to the Indians. His son, however, believed that the Indians had to openly protest against the British to gain independence for India. When Jawaharlal began to sympathize

*Jawaharlal and his parents,
Motilal and Swarprani
Nehru, circa 1899*

with the faint stirrings of Indian independence, Motilal berated him. "I do not approve of your politics," his father wrote him. The opinions of the Nehru family were important because the Nehrus were one of the wealthiest families in India. Motilal was a successful lawyer who could easily afford to keep his family in luxury. For example, he provided the family with a beautiful and exotic home, named Anand Bhavan, in the city of Praya-graj (formerly Allahabad) in northern India. The estate was filled with lush gardens, fruit trees, and tropical birds. Dozens of bedrooms, an indoor swimming pool, and tennis courts added to a lifestyle that was rare in India.

Motilal Nehru had been educated in England and had adopted many English ways. He filled Anand Bhavan with fine linens, furniture, and china from Europe. He hired English governesses to instruct his family and servants in the English language. He owned several expensive cars from Europe and entertained English and American diplomats on a regular basis. The Nehru household followed the British customs of afternoon tea and the cultivation of beautiful rose gardens.

Like her grandfather, Indira's father was also educated in England and became a successful lawyer in Prayagraj. By the time Jawaharlal returned to India, he was twenty-two years old—a good age to marry and start a family. Like most marriages in India at the time, Jawaharlal's marriage was arranged, so the bride and groom had no choice in the matter. Arranged marriages are an old tradition still found in many cultures.

Looks were important to Motilal. A young woman named Kamala was described as "dazzlingly beautiful," so Motilal selected her to be his son's wife. She was given in marriage to Jawaharlal when she was sixteen years old. As was customary, the bride and groom did not see each other until the wedding day.

When Kamala learned that she was to marry Jawaharlal, she knew that she had to learn English. Everyone in the Nehru household spoke English. If she was to fit in with the other members of the family, she had to be able to communicate with them. So with the help of an English tutor, Kamala quickly learned to speak and understand a little English.

Indian families often consisted of parents, grandparents, aunts, uncles, and children all living under the same roof. The Nehru family was no exception. Kamala moved in with her husband's family, as was the custom, but the family did not accept her. Kamala's mother-in-law and sister-in-law took a dislike to her. They found fault with everything Kamala did, and

Jawaharlal with Kamala on their wedding day

they lied about her to Motilal and Jawaharlal so they would dislike her and find her unworthy as a wife. Kamala, however, bore all of this mistreatment and mistrust silently, maintaining her dignity and poise. In Indian society, it was unthinkable that a wife would talk back to or even defend herself against her husband's family. Kamala, trying to fulfill her duties as a good Indian wife, quietly bore her anger and disappointment until she was alone in her room. There, she could let her tears flow freely.

Jawaharlal found his marriage to Kamala to be one of custom and convenience rather than a sincere desire to have an intimate relationship. He didn't have much time for his wife, and when he was home, he didn't pay much attention to her. His political aspirations grew stronger after returning home to India, and he became passionately involved in Indian politics.

Indira's birth in 1917 did not help the situation. Her birth, like that of most females born into Indian families, was not heralded with excitement. Indira's grandmother was disappointed that the child was not a male. Fortunately for Indira, Motilal did not share her feelings. He scolded Swaruprani, saying: "This daughter of Jawaharlal, for all you know, may prove better than a thousand sons."

Since Motilal was the head of the family, his opinion set the standard for the rest of the household. He also had the honor of naming his granddaughter. He named her "Indira" after his mother. Indira's parents then added the name Priyadarshini, which means "dear to behold." She was later nicknamed Indu and became her grandfather's pride and joy.

In addition to Indira's family, another person played an important role, not only in the life of the Nehrus, but also in the life of India. His name was Mohandas Karamchand

Gandhi, third from right, *was a lawyer in South Africa while in his early twenties.*

Gandhi. When the Nehru family met Gandhi, they were struck by the powerful presence of a man who was so small that he looked as if a strong wind would knock him over. Gandhiji, as his followers called him, was quickly becoming India's leader in its struggle for independence. (Indians often add the suffix "-iji" to a name as a term of affection. It means "dearest one.")

A short, wizened man, Mohandas Gandhi was a poor Indian lawyer who had learned about the seriousness of racial prejudice in South Africa. In 1893, while riding on a train in South Africa, he encountered a situation that changed his life forever. On that particular day, a white man was ushered into the compartment where Gandhi was sitting. The white passenger told the train conductor that Gandhi could not sit in the first-class section. The conductor, deferring to the white man, threw Gandhi off the train at the next station.

A large Indian population had settled in South Africa to work the tea and coffee plantations, but the white South Africans looked down upon them. Indians were not allowed to vote or own property. They had to pay enormous taxes and were required to carry special identification at all times.

Gandhi began his campaign for Indian reform in South Africa by holding meetings and teaching his fellow Indians how to lobby for their rights in a peaceful manner. He developed a method of direct social action based upon the principles of courage, nonviolence, and truth, which he called *satyagraha*. Satyagraha meant that people, as a group,

Mohandas Gandhi in 1908

peacefully refuse to obey the unjust laws and restrictions imposed on them by a government.

Finally in 1914, the South African government reached an agreement with Gandhi by passing the Indian Relief Act, which legalized non-Christian marriages and abolished some of the taxes that laborers paid. These concessions were temporary, however. When Gandhi returned to India in 1915, the South African government reneged on all the promises it had made.

Upon arriving home, Gandhi planned to put satyagraha into effect in India. He believed that if the method worked against the South African government, it could also be effective against the British in India. Within five years, he became the leader of the Indian nationalist movement.

Gandhi's first step after arriving in India was to set up an *ashram*, or community. He then invited the lowest Indian caste—the untouchables—to join. Gandhi rallied against the caste system, believing that all people are equal. When he invited the lowest caste to join his community, he caused an uproar, but he also made a point. He would not tolerate prejudice and bigotry, and he insisted that if the Indian people wanted their independence, they had to fight for it as a unified whole. The people gave Gandhi the title "Mahatma," or "Great Soul," because of his compassion for all human life.

Indira first met Mohandas Gandhi when she was just a toddler. At the invitation of Indira's father, Gandhi visited at Anand Bhavan often. Motilal liked and respected Gandhi, but he initially disliked his philosophy of "peaceful resistance." It was unthinkable that an upper-caste lawyer with his lifestyle and success would even think about breaking the law. The passionate interest with which Jawaharlal listened and responded to Gandhi's impassioned speeches made Motilal uncomfortable.

In 1919, however, something happened that caused Motilal to change his mind about independence. The British government introduced new laws that made it illegal to organize opposition to the government. Gandhi knew that people were upset, but he encouraged them to go on strike and demonstrate peacefully. Thousands of men, women, and children gathered in Jallianwalla Bagh, an open area that had once been a garden, for a demonstration against the new restrictions that the British government had imposed on them. The British considered this demonstration to be illegal and sent the army to intervene.

A British officer had his soldiers seal off the exits to the park, then he ordered his soldiers to fire on the unarmed crowd. Almost four hundred people were killed, and at least twelve hundred more were badly wounded. The soldiers stopped firing only because they ran out of bullets after 1,650 rounds.

Indira was only two years old when the massacre at the park took place. Her father was on the committee appointed to investigate what had happened. When Jawaharlal and Motilal arrived at the park, they were sickened by what they saw. Motilal finally understood the extent of British imperialism and thought it was brutal and uncivilized. Both father and son vowed that they would do whatever was necessary to make sure that India won independence.

Motilal and Jawaharlal began their crusade by gathering together other supporters of India's independence. They gave talks and held rallies to stir the passion of the Indian people. The British government, however, soon recognized that Motilal and his son were capable of causing an Indian uprising and knew that these two influential men had to be stopped.

After witnessing the massacre at Jallianwalla Bagh, Jawaharlal, left, and Motilal, right, joined Gandhi's nonviolent disobedience campaign.

Arrest and imprisonment became a way of life for the Nehru family. In 1921 five-year-old Indira sat on Motilal's lap in court and heard the judge sentence her father and grandfather to six months in prison. When she arrived home after bidding a tearful farewell to the beloved men in her life, Indira found soldiers raiding her home. They confiscated furniture, cars, and silverware while Indira and her mother looked on, helpless to stop them. Indira later wrote, "The tension was not only due to prison terms, but when my parents were fined they didn't pay the fine, it was a policy, [of the Indian Congress] so the police used to come and take any bit of property in lieu of the fine and quite often—in fact always—they took much more than the fine."

The constant disruption in the Nehru household caused tension for the other members of Indira's family. Her aunts, uncles, and grandmother felt that it was unfair for the weight of India's independence to fall on the shoulders of the Nehru family. Family members criticized Motilal and Jawaharlal, and Indira resented the family's lack of support. Consequently, she became very independent and protective of her parents and grandparents and openly resented any critical talk about her father or grandfather. Even at such an early age, Indira felt compelled to speak her mind when she thought that an injustice was being done.

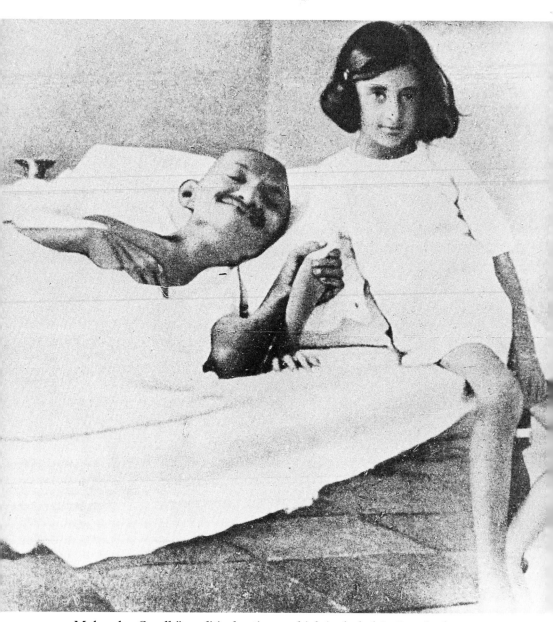

Mohandas Gandhi's political actions, which included fasting, had tremendous influence on the Nehru family, including Indira.

 TWO

Amidst the Burning Cloth

1922–1926

One morning in 1922, when Indira was five years old, she awoke to the smell of smoke. The little girl thought the house was on fire, and she ran down the hall to the front porch. There, on the lawn in front of her house, was a huge bonfire. Indira smiled as she remembered what her mother had told her the night before. She had explained to Indira that, in protest against the British government, all Indians had agreed to follow a suggestion that Gandhi put forth. Gandhi told the Indians that if they really wanted to demonstrate to the British how they felt about Indian independence, they had to stop buying foreign goods. He suggested that they burn all their foreign possessions, including their clothes, and start weaving their own cloth for their garments.

The Nehrus, who probably owned more British goods than most Indians, decided to display their intentions publicly. Servants and family members threw furniture, drapes, cloth, rugs, and clothing into the fire. They wore garments made of rough, homespun cotton cloth, called *khadi*, which they had made themselves. This cloth was irritating to the skin and often caused rashes and bleeding. Yet the Indian people were determined that as long as the British ruled their country, they would never again buy anything from England.

The fire had been burning for two days when Indira was asked to contribute to the cause. She didn't mind giving up her pretty dresses and wearing the uncomfortable cloth, but she was particularly fond of a favorite English doll.

Looking back on those days, Indira wrote, "For days on end—or was it weeks? it doesn't matter, it seemed an eternity—I was overwhelmed by the burden of decision—the struggle went on between love for my doll, pride of owning

Mohandas Gandhi at the spinning wheel, circa 1931. He led the movement to boycott British clothing and other goods, in favor of Indian-made clothes.

such a lovely thing, and what I thought to be my duty towards my country. . . . At last I made my decision and, quivering with tension, I took the doll up on the roof-terrace and set fire to it. Then the tears came as if they would never stop and for some days I was ill with a temperature. To this day I hate striking a match."

While Indira's father and grandfather whiled away their days in jail, reading, writing letters, and spinning khadi on a spinning wheel, she played her political fantasy games in the safety of her home. Instead of the usual childhood themes of marriage and family, Indira's games always got intensely political. Her dolls were—at the same time—British, with tiny pith helmets, and Indian, wearing khadi and the small white cap that became known as the Gandhi cap. In Indira's scenarios, the dolls fought against each other or argued their issues aloud. Her dollouse became a shop that refused to go along with Gandhi's request for simplicity and still sold foreign goods. Her dolls, dressed in white khadi, would picket the store, as Indira had seen her mother and aunts do so often. She devised weapons, guns and clubs, and put them in the hands of her dolls to represent the British militia and the police. As Indira grew older, however, she tired of her make-believe political ambitions. Indira wanted to do something real, to make something happen.

In 1924, Gandhi organized a *sangha*, or group, that was dedicated to traveling throughout India, urging people to take the first step toward independence by making their own clothes. Indira often accompanied her mother and aunts on these sangha trips, and this experience deepened her commitment to a free India.

For the first eight years of Indira's life, her education consisted both of real life experiences and of stories from the

Hindu culture. Two Hindu epics, *Ramayana* and *Mahabharata*, were endlessly recounted by her great aunt Rajvati. Indira's mother took care of her spiritual education by encouraging her young daughter to join her in Hindu prayers and chants. Unlike her husband, Kamala was a deeply spiritual person, and she inspired Indira with her unshakable faith and courage.

The subject of proper schooling for Indira was a touchy one in the Nehru household. Jawaharlal first sent her to an Indian public school, the Modern School, near their home in Prayagraj. But Motilal disagreed and took advantage of the fact that his son was in jail and couldn't do more than protest. Believing Indira would get a better education at a private school, Motilal sent her to St. Cecilia's, a British school. Jawaharlal strongly disapproved, fearing that the English would unduly influence his daughter. Indira was then pulled out of school and given private tutors. This change in her education didn't seem to bother her very much, since she had never felt comfortable with the other children in school anyway.

In 1926, when Indira was nine years old, Kamala was diagnosed with tuberculosis, a disease of the lungs and respiratory system. Although tuberculosis is curable with modern antibiotics, it was a common cause of death at the time. The doctors suggested that Jawaharlal take her to Switzerland, where she could receive specialized medical treatment. One of the first things Jawaharlal did after arriving in Switzerland was to enroll Indira in L'Ecole Internationale, a Swiss international school. That year was one of the happiest of Indira's life. The time in Geneva gave Indira increased independence. She had to go to the market and deal with foreign shopkeepers who had a different culture and tradition. Indira found that she could take charge of her life and take care of her mother, too, when needed. And when she was in school, she sat in classrooms with nearly seventy-five students of varying nationalities.

The school, situated in a Swiss chalet in the mountains, was never boring. The children did their morning lessons and spent the afternoons in the country learning gymnastics, dancing, and gardening. Indira was always fond of nature, and L' Ecole Internationale developed this interest even further.

On most days, Jawaharlal walked his daughter to and from school. For Indira and her father, these were special times when they could share their thoughts and ideas. More often than not, their conversation focused on politics and the future of India. Indira told her father of her desire to take a greater part in Indian politics. She saw herself as an Indian Joan of Arc, one who would sacrifice herself and do whatever it took to make India independent. Jawaharlal felt a deep pride in his daughter but cautioned her about her age. He also thought that she was being a bit too idealistic, hoping to achieve by herself what an entire nation couldn't accomplish.

As a young girl, Indira was already thinking of ways to help India gain independence from Great Britain.

 THREE

Indira's Monkey Brigade

1927–1933

After a one-year stay, the Swiss doctors allowed Kamala's return to India. In 1927, when Indira was ten years old, she and her parents sailed home to India. Before going to Prayagraj, they went to Madras to attend a session of the Indian National Congress. Motilal was president of the Congress, and it was very important that the family show their support. Besides, Jawaharlal had been out of the country for a year, and he missed being in the thick of political activity.

Upon arriving home, Indira was promptly enrolled in St. Mary's Convent School in Prayagraj. She was very unhappy there and felt that consequently she didn't learn very much. The English teachers frequently scolded the students and seemed to single out Indira for frequent criticism. While she attended school, Indira was also being tutored at home in Hindi, the language of India and Hinduism, the major religion of her country.

Indira's father was once again in prison, and this time the police had physically abused him. He had been leading a demonstration when a police officer on horseback, carrying a six-foot metal-tipped pole, began beating Jawaharlal and the other demonstrators.

Although Indira was only twelve, she wanted desperately to join the Congress Party with her parents. Members had to be eighteen years old, however. Indira invented a solution to her problem with Vanar Sena or the "Monkey Brigade." Indira's choice of a name was derived from a story in the Indian epic poem *Ramayana*, a story most Indian children knew. In this story, an army of monkeys helped Rama, the hero, conquer Ravan, the demon-king of Lanka. Indira probably likened the demon-king to the British rulers and the army of monkeys to the Monkey Brigade.

More than one thousand children attended the first meeting of the Monkey Brigade. At first, Kamala and Jawaharlal were amused by Indira's attempt to take part in the country's political life. Before long, however, they realized that these children could serve an important function in the fight for independence. The Monkey Brigade sewed and hung national flags, brought food and drink to people who marched or attended rallies, wrote letters for prisoners who didn't know how to write, and gave first aid to Congress volunteers injured by police brutality.

One of the young people who got involved with Indira and her political activities was a young man named Feroze Gandhi. (Feroze was not related to Mohandas Gandhi. Gandhi is a common name in India.) Feroze and Indira became very close friends. He was as passionate about the freedom movement as Indira, and this was their major bond. Most members of the Nehru family liked Feroze,

As his fellow marchers look on, Mohandas Gandhi defies the Salt Laws.

and he became a frequent and welcome visitor at Anand Bhavan.

In 1929, Indira's father was elected president of the Indian Congress. One of Jawaharlal's first acts as president was to draft a resolution proclaiming that *purna swaraj*, or complete independence, was the goal of the Congress and the people of India.

In April 1930, Mohandas Gandhi led another peaceful demonstration. The British had enacted salt laws in India, forbidding citizens from extracting salt from seawater. If the Indian people wanted salt, they had to purchase it from government agencies. On March 12, Gandhi began a twenty-three-day march to the small seacoast village of Dandi. On April 6, Gandhi, along with thousands of followers, spent the night in prayer. In the morning, he led the multitude into the sea and, in total disregard for the law, began to collect salt-water in evaporation pans. Gandhi and thousands of others were arrested in a bloody confrontation with the police. Jawaharlal was arrested in April and Motilal in June for their part in the salt protest.

Indira had left St. Mary's by this time, and she spent her time educating herself by reading. She had always been a voracious reader and sometimes got so absorbed in her books that she would forget to eat. The library at Anand Bhavan boasted a collection of nearly six thousand books, and her father was constantly adding new ones. Before visiting him in prison, she would often write him a letter, asking him to have a new list of books ready for her.

When Indira wasn't reading or working in the Monkey Brigade, she was running. Jawaharlal taught her that exercise was the way to keep both body and mind healthy. This practice probably helped Indira remain strong and centered during difficult situations, such as having family members imprisoned.

Indira was somewhat used to her father and grandfather spending time in prison, but on New Year's Day in 1931, she was forced to deal with an exceptionally difficult situation. Indira's family was having dinner when the phone rang. Indira gave her account of the event: "I went to take it and it was a warning; they just said that Mrs. Nehru would be arrested the next morning. Before I could reply they put down the phone and we didn't find out who called. I went and told her. She said a lot had to be done before her arrest. She called a meeting of prominent Congress workers and in the meantime, she asked me to pack for her. Since she thought the house might also be searched, we had to get rid of certain papers. . . . She was arrested at about 5 A.M."

Indira was stunned. Her father was in prison, and her grandfather was showing signs of age and illness since his release from prison the previous September. Indira felt alone and sad. Although her aunts and cousins were in the house, Indira missed her parents.

Kamala remained in prison at Lucknow for twenty-six days. By the end of January, it was obvious that Motilal was close to death, so the British officials sent Kamala home and released Jawaharlal from the prison at Naini. The family gathered at Prayagraj to support Motilal in his final days.

On February 5, 1931, Motilal died. Indira was devastated by the event. All of India was in deep mourning for Motilal Nehru, but no one felt the sadness as deeply as the two people who were closest to him, Indira and her father.

Motilal's body was wrapped in the Indian flag and laid on a funeral pyre, as is the custom in India. There is no burial of the dead, only cremation. Then, when his body was only ash, the remains were carried to the Ganges River, considered sacred to the Indians, and the ashes were scattered upon the water. Jawaharlal later wrote that "as evening fell on the river bank on that winter day... Gandhi said a few moving words to the multitude, and then all of us crept silently home. The stars were out and shining brightly when we returned, lonely and desolate."

In June 1931, Indira traveled to Ceylon (present-day Sri Lanka) with her parents. Perhaps there was a need to get away from the desolate mood at Anand Bhavan after Motilal's death. They spent about a month in Ceylon touring the island and visiting the historic sites. Since most of the inhabitants were Buddhists, Jawaharlal instructed his daughter on Buddhism and the life of Siddhartha Gautama, the founder of the religion. The title Buddha means "Enlightened One."

Kamala's poor health had deteriorated while in the harsh confines of her prison cell. By the end of 1931, her doctors sent her to a sanitarium in northern India to recuperate.

Knowing that he could be arrested again and sent to prison at any time, Jawaharlal worried about Indira being left alone at Anand Bhavan. He had learned of an unusual school located in Poona, almost one thousand miles from Prayagraj. He sent Indira there just before being arrested again. The school curriculum, directed by a young couple, Jehengir and Coonverbai Vakil, combined ancient Indian methods of teaching and modern Western systems.

Indira, standing second from right, *poses with her family. Nehru family members were in and out of prison most of Indira's young life, so gatherings of this size were rare.*

The Poona school was housed in an old bungalow. The Vakils occupied one room, while the dozen or so girls slept in the other three rooms. Each morning the sleeping mats had to be put away so that the bedrooms could be converted into classrooms.

The meals were simple and the girls were disciplined daily by Mrs. Vakil. Indira, now fourteen years old, was the oldest in the school, and without any friends her age she felt lonely and worried. She knew that her father was back in prison and that her mother was not well.

The only way Indira could deal with these stresses and strains was to keep busy. She took the opportunity to learn many art forms from the talented Mrs. Vakil. Indira learned batik, or the dyeing of cloth, dancing, and drama. She became secretary of the Literary Society and helped with the choral productions at the school.

After she was at the school for a few months, Indira also became responsible for her three younger cousins, who were sent to the school after their mother, Indira's aunt Vijayalakshmi (Nan, to the family), was arrested and imprisoned. Because the children were scared and sad to be away from home, Indira felt that it was her responsibility to help them adjust to their new life.

Some time after that, Mrs. Vakil decided to accept several children into the school who were members of the untouchable caste. Indira now had the additional daily task of washing and feeding these young children.

By August 1932, Mohandas Gandhi had already spent ten months in jail. His imprisonments were becoming more frequent because he was continually expressing a philosophy contrary to that of the British government's. Gandhi believed in "India for the Indians." He used every opportunity to make his views heard, and he went to any length—even at the sacrifice of his own health—to get the British to listen to what he said. In September 1932, the British government established a Government's Communal Award. Unlike most awards, this was not a reward for doing something great. This award was a document stating that religious communities, which included Hindus, Sikhs, Christians, and Muslims, could only elect those of their own faith to represent them in the legislature. Gandhi saw this as a move by the British to create further disparity among the various religions. He announced from his prison cell that he would fast until he died or until the British changed the law.

From his prison cell, Jawaharlal wrote about this news to his daughter. He was grief-stricken by the thought that he might lose his mentor, or spiritual teacher, and he was helpless to do anything. Indira decided to take matters into her own hands. She gathered the children at her school together and explained Gandhi's situation. Indira and the children held a day-long fast—from one morning to the following morning without eating anything—to show support for Gandhi's fast.

Gandhi was in a prison just a few miles from her school, so with her three cousins in hand, Indira traveled to see him. When she arrived at the prison, Indira told the guard that she was Nehru's daughter and demanded to see Gandhi. When she and the children were finally escorted to his prison cell, she sat on the floor with him and told him about their one-day fast. Indira also told him that they were all praying for him.

Gandhi was delighted with Indira's visit and the children's efforts. He even remarked that Indira must have been eating better at the school than at Anand Bhavan because he was finally seeing signs of fullness on her bony frame. Four days later, Gandhi ended his fast because the government, under pressure by the Indian people, retracted the most objectionable parts of the award.

A twenty-year-old Indira smiles for the camera in Mumbai.

 FOUR

A Young Woman in a Turbulent World

1934–1940

Jawaharlal was finally released from prison in September 1933. He immediately traveled to Poona to see Gandhi and Indira. The children at the school liked Nehru and were impressed that they were sitting with one of the most prominent Indian leaders of their country. Jawaharlal told stories to the children and helped devise small toys for them. When he left after a week, Indira was sad to see him go.

Later that year, when Indira was sixteen years old, she graduated from the Poona school and continued her education at Shantineketan, an informal university located in Bengal. The school was founded by Rabindranath Tagore, a philosopher, poet, and mystic who had won the Nobel Prize for Literature in 1913. Before Indira left for her first semester at Shantineketan, however, she traveled to Kashmir in northwestern India for the summer. Her mother, partially recovered from her illness, and Mr. and Mrs. Ranjit Pandit, Indira's aunt and uncle, traveled together. Mr. Pandit was a scholar, and he was in Kashmir conducting research for a book he was writing.

*Poet and philosopher
Rabindranath Tagore
founded the school Indira
attended at Shantineketan.*

Indira accompanied her uncle to many ancient historic sites in Kashmir. She thought that Kashmir was the most beautiful place she had ever seen. After visiting Kashmir, Indira and Kamala went to Kolkata in eastern India to visit Jawaharlal in prison. They then went to the Ramakrishna Mission at Belur, near Kolkata. This was a Hindu ashram, and Indira and her mother spent many days peacefully sitting by the river and focusing on their own thoughts.

Indira made an important decision at the mission. Her friend, Feroze, had asked her to marry him. She had told him that she would give him her answer before she left for school. Staying at the ashram gave Indira the opportunity to put her thoughts and feelings in order, and she made a decision. She would tell Feroze no.

The school at Shantineketan was somewhat familiar to Indira because the school in Poona had been modeled on Tagore's school. The administrators of the school were surprised that Indira, who came from a wealthy family, could so easily adapt to the somewhat simple life of the school. But her stay at Poona had prepared her for Shantineketan.

The students arose at four o'clock in the morning, washed their clothes and cleaned their rooms. Tagore took an intense interest in how his school was run, and he was always there, watching the children and guiding their lives.

Indira found companionship at Shantineketan with students her own age. This was a new experience for her, and she reveled in the emotional and intellectual communication she shared with her peers. She continued to read extensively, but she found that she suddenly took equal delight in other activities, such as Indian classical dancing and painting. However, one of the most important aspects of Shantineketan, at least for Indira, was the peacefulness and tranquility that the school encouraged.

The students started and ended each day with silent meditation. Silence was kept whenever possible, broken only by the sweet, melodious singing of Tagore's poems in Bengali, one of the loveliest Indian languages, or the delightful sounds of forest birds in the garden. This tranquil atmosphere was such a healthy change for Indira that she remarked, "I seemed suddenly to have landed in another world."

A few months after Indira began her studies at Shantineketan, her mother again became very ill and was sent to the Bhowali Sanatorium in the Himalaya Mountains. In 1935, Kamala's health had deteriorated so severely that Indira was asked to accompany her mother to Europe for a cure. Kamala traveled to Lausanne, Switzerland, where she died on February 28, 1936. A sorrowful Jawaharlal, who had been released from prison, was at Kamala's side.

The death of her mother was a severe blow for Indira. It had been only five years since her grandfather had died. Indira felt alone in the world. Her mother and grandfather were dead, and she never knew when her father would be returned to prison. The question of her future and her continuing education was one that both she and her father discussed at length, but in the end, Indira made the final decision. She would go to England. Both her grandfather and father had received an excellent education in England, and Indira knew that Feroze was studying at the London School of Economics.

In 1937 Indira passed the entrance exam for Somerville College at Oxford. There she took courses in history, public and social administration, and anthropology. As was her habit, Indira also read widely about other subjects such as art, archaeology, architecture, and comparative religions. She joined the student wing of the British Labour Party, which encouraged students to become active in politics.

One day, V. K. Krishna Menon, a friend of her father, approached Indira and asked her to go with him to a gathering of social activists. She wasn't supposed to leave Oxford, but she decided to break the rules. When they arrived at Caxton Hall, someone noticed that she was in the audience and announced that Miss Nehru was going to speak. Indira later revealed, "I was terrified, especially since the hall was so big. . . . I just couldn't get out any sound! Finally I managed to say something; but there was a drunk in the room who said: 'She doesn't speak, she squeaks.' This, of course, brought the

The death of Kamala, shown here with Jawaharlal in 1931, was a tremendous loss for Indira.

house down and I vowed that I would never, never speak in public again." Although Indira was happy at Oxford, she longed to be back home in India with her father. She felt that she should be helping her country realize its dream of independence rather than sitting in a classroom listening to lectures.

Indira became ill with pleurisy, an illness that is usually caused by an infection in the lungs that brings chest pain and coughing. She was sent to Switzerland after her second term at Oxford and then returned to England. She was more homesick than ever. Trouble was brewing in Europe, and war was expected to break out any day. Indira knew that if that happened, she would find it difficult to return to India.

As it was, she waited too long to make her decision to leave England. The German dictator Adolf Hitler had invaded Austria in 1938, then Poland in 1939. World War II had begun, and Europe was in confusion.

Indira was there in London during the beginning of the blitz, the German air attacks on England which began in 1940. She joined the Red Cross as a volunteer and spent several weeks driving an ambulance and tending to air-raid victims. She soon realized that England was too dangerous; she wanted to go home. Feroze decided to travel with her, so they set out on a ship which took a long journey around the Cape of Good Hope at the southern tip of Africa.

While visiting Cape Town, South Africa, Indira was again asked to speak at a reception. Remembering her painfully embarrassing experience at Caxton Hall, Indira was very reluctant, but she felt obligated at least to attend the event, since the South Africans were making such a fuss over Nehru's daughter. Nehru, an important leader of the Indian freedom movement, had recently been elected president of the Congress Party.

After visiting an area where black African railway workers lived, Indira changed her mind about speaking. "The conditions were so terrible," she wrote later, "that I got worked up." At the reception, when it was announced that Miss Nehru wouldn't speak, Indira banged the table and said,

"I do wish to speak." The chairman was startled, but before he could say anything, Indira went to the microphone. She pleaded with the white audience, saying, "You must come to an understanding with the Africans . . . because . . . it is they who will [one day] rule this country. And then what will your descendants do?"

Mohandas Gandhi greets Indira. She often visited Gandhi on her father's behalf.

 FIVE

A Rebel for the Cause

1941–1944

In March 1941, when twenty-four-year-old Indira arrived in Mumbai on the west coast of India, no family members were there to greet her, no well-wishers happy for her safe return. Her father was once again in prison, along with many other Indians.

World War II was raging throughout Europe and Asia, but the Indians seemed almost oblivious to what was happening outside their own country. Their only focus was independence, and the problems of the rest of the world didn't concern them.

One highlight brightened Indira's return, however. Gandhi had wired her in Mumbai requesting that Indira go to see him. Indira traveled to Sevagram in Prayagraj, Gandhi's ashram. After the somewhat mild temperatures in Europe, Indira felt suffocated by the intense heat. Moreover, when she arrived at the ashram, Indira was astonished and annoyed by the chaos and upheaval surrounding a man who the country beheld as a peacemaker. The turbulence, however, was not caused by Gandhi, but by his followers.

They were all fighting over who would carry his food to him, who would serve him, who would clean for him and do his washing, who would sit where when he was talking, and so on. Indira finally got tired of the petty quarrels and traveled to Dehra Dun to see her father in prison. He told her that he was going to be released in a few days, and she told him that she had to discuss something of great importance when he finally returned home. She was going to announce her intention to get married.

When she finally told Jawaharlal about her plans, Indira was disappointed that her news was not met with the usual excitement that most announcements of this kind would elicit. Jawaharlal was not unhappy that Indira wanted to marry, but that she wanted to marry Feroze.

Although the Nehru family had known and liked Feroze for many years, they felt that he was not a fit candidate for Indira. The Nehrus were Brahmans, the highest of the Indian castes, and they were Hindus. (Feroze's family were Parsis, a small religious sect that originally came to India from Persia—and therefore are not considered "true" Indians.) Feroze was proud of his lower-middle-class background, but the Nehrus were aristocrats. Jawaharlal's objections to his daughter's marriage were based more on class considerations than on religious grounds.

Jawaharlal wanted to stop the marriage if possible. He gave Indira the usual fatherly advice about not rushing into marriage, giving herself a chance to meet other eligible young men, and warning her that her affection for Feroze might just stem from the fact that he filled a loneliness gap when she was in Europe.

Jawaharlal's concerns were that Feroze was poor, that he wouldn't be able to provide Indira with the lifestyle she had

Gandhi attracted many followers while striving for India's independence.

been accustomed to, and that Feroze wouldn't make her happy because of the differences in their personalities. Indira was reserved and often retreated into herself, while Feroze was gregarious and impulsive.

These arguments bore no weight as far as Indira was concerned, however. She was adamant. She didn't care about caste and religion when it came to Feroze. She only saw that he had been her support at difficult times during her life, that he had been with her while caring for her mother in Switzerland, that he shared her political activism and passion for Indian independence, and that he loved her. Indira was determined to marry him. She even told her father that she would not talk to him ever again if he did not approve the marriage. Jawaharlal finally gave his approval, and the date was set for March 26, 1942.

Indira and Feroze were married at Anand Bhavan. A sacred fire was lit in the main room of the house, and the marriage took place around it. Indira began the ceremony by sitting next to her father and ended it by taking a new seat next to her husband. As is customary, Indira and Feroze took seven steps around the fire while repeating ancient Sanskrit words:

> By taking seven steps with me do thou
>   become my friend.
> By taking seven steps together we become friends.
> I shall become thy friend.
> I shall never give up thy friendship.
> Do thou never give up my friendship.
> Let us live together and take counsel of one
>   another.

Indira and Feroze in front of the sacred fire at their wedding ceremony in 1942

Indira and Feroze were then tied together with a scarf and showered with rose petals. After the wedding, the hundreds of guests from Prayagraj society and the Indian Congress joined the newly married couple in a wedding breakfast, followed by music and dancing. The wedding was a refreshing respite for all who attended. It allowed them a joyful break from the turbulence of their political lives. Their rest would be short lived, however.

Two months later, Gandhi launched the slogan, "Quit India." This was their final declaration to the British. It was the Indian way of saying, "Get out. We want our country back!"

Congress workers—party members and volunteers—spread the words "Quit India" all over the country. They wrote the slogan on British buses and on city walls. Riots broke out frequently, and Indians attacked British police and families.

Indira decided to use Feroze, who was light in complexion and could pass for a British citizen, as a courier. He further disguised himself by growing a beard and moustache and by wearing British clothes. With his help, Indira was able to pass money and political literature to the Congress workers who had developed an underground system.

In September of 1942, Indira addressed a rally in Prayagraj while Feroze watched from the window of their small two-room apartment in Tagore Town. The British soldiers had gotten word that there would be a meeting. Feroze watched from a distance until he saw a British police sergeant threaten Indira with a bayonet. Impulsively, he ran to his wife's side, only to be arrested along with her. They were tried and imprisoned, along with hundreds of other people.

Prison, for Indira, was an eye-opening experience. For years she had been in and out of prisons—but only as a visitor. She later wrote, "What a world of difference there is between hearing and seeing from the outside and the actual experience. No one who has not been in prison for any length of time can ever visualize the numbness of spirit that can creep over one."

Some prisoners were allowed certain privileges, but not Indira. Perhaps the only comfort was that Feroze was in the same prison, and after much pleading, they were finally allowed to see one another for a short time. Then Feroze was transferred to another prison some distance away.

Indira tried to keep her spirits up by reading, talking to the other prisoners, and helping a young mother who had a small baby with her. Finally, after eight months, Indira was released on May 13, 1943. Feroze was released in August. Indira writes of her release, "My unexpected release was like coming suddenly out of a dark passage. I was dazzled with the rush of life, the many hues and textures, the scale of sounds and the range of ideas. Just to touch and listen was a disturbing experience and it took a while to get adjusted to normal living."

Jawaharlal had also been in prison. He had been arrested along with the entire Congress Working Committee, the policy-making body. Almost the entire Nehru family was in prison except for Indira's two teenage cousins and a servant who stayed in Anand Bhavan. Indira's Aunt Krishna had stayed out of the political arena because she had two small children, but her husband was in prison. The Japanese, who were also fighting against the British during World War II, were threatening to invade India, and the British were scared. They would no longer tolerate civil disobedience of any kind, and anyone who tried it spent time in prison.

By December 1943, Indira realized that she was pregnant. She was thrilled. One of the reasons she had married was to have children. Indira went to Mumbai to stay with her aunt. On August 20, 1944, Indira gave birth to a healthy boy, whom she named Rajiv Ratna. "I think it was one of the most joyful moments in my life," she wrote, "although I must say at that time he seemed quite ugly. . . . But to a woman, motherhood is the highest fulfillment. To bring a new being into this world, to see its perfection and to dream of its future greatness is the most moving of all experiences and fills one with wonder and exaltation."

Jawaharlal displays the national flag of independent India.

 SIX

An Independent India

1945–1948

In 1945 World War II ended, and India was on the verge of winning its long awaited independence. Winston Churchill, the British prime minister, had been opposed to India gaining independence, but in July 1945, his party lost the election to Clement Attlee of the Labour Party. Mr. Attlee made the issue of India's independence a priority. The first thing he did after taking office was to free all political prisoners. Indira's father was going home after spending a total of nine years in prison.

Indira had been concentrating on being a mother and wife since the birth of Rajiv. Having had such a difficult childhood herself, Indira was anxious to give her son lots of love and attention. She believed that the amount of time spent with children didn't matter as much as the quality of that time. Indira knew that she would eventually return to the political arena, but at this time motherhood was her priority.

Indira knew that real education is the training of mind and body in order to produce a balanced personality. She also believed that formal education could only take a child so far. She believed it was a mother's responsibility to develop self-discipline and strong character in her children.

*In 1946 riots broke out in Kolkata between Muslims and Hindus,
destroying parts of the city and causing numerous deaths.*

In April 1946, Indira found that she was again pregnant.
She and Feroze hoped for a girl, and both were convinced that
they would have a daughter.

In July 1946, Jawaharlal went to Delhi and asked Indira
to join him there to help him during this period of political tur-
moil. He had been elected president of the Indian Congress,
and there was a movement to separate India into two states,
a Hindu India and a Muslim state called Pakistan.

This picture of a fractured India greatly disturbed Jawaharlal. His vision was one of a united India, with no divisions of caste or religion. Some other members of the Congress, however, did not agree with him. They believed that India should be all Hindu, since Hindus comprised 85 percent of the country's population.

The British government agreed with Gandhi and Jawaharlal that India should remain one state, but the wishes of the Muslims prevailed. On August 14, 1946, Muslims rioted against their Hindu neighbors. People who had lived side by side in peace became bitter rivals. Muslims slaughtered whole villages, and in retaliation many Hindus turned against innocent Muslim families.

Gandhi, even in the face of violence, refused to accept a divided India. He toured those parts of the country where the violence was rampant and tried to bring the Muslims and Hindus to a peaceful compromise. He then began a fast, hoping to stop the bloodshed. But neighbors were still killing neighbors, and thousands of people were dead.

The British were trying to establish the borders of Pakistan and India, hoping that would stop the violence. Pakistan was divided into East Pakistan and West Pakistan, with a large part of northern India in the middle. Once the territories were fixed, however, an additional problem arose. Some Muslims found themselves in India, and some Hindus found themselves in the newly established country of Pakistan. A mass migration took place, with more than thirteen million Indians leaving their homes. Indian Muslims went north to Pakistan, and Indian Hindus traveled south to India. Families traveled on foot, carrying their possessions in bundles on their backs.

On December 14, 1946, Indira gave birth to a second son, Sanjay. But less than two months later, she was back in the political arena. She and Jawaharlal tried to help establish peace between Muslims and Hindus. Gandhi asked Indira to visit Muslim communities and report back to him.

Indira traveled to Mussoorie to work in the refugee camps there. One day, while on her way home, she had an experience she wouldn't forget. As she was returning home, she saw a man being chased by hundreds of people. Indira told the driver to stop, but he refused. She told him that she would jump out if he didn't stop. He still refused but slowed down considerably. "I had taken off my *chappals* [shoes]," she later wrote, "so, I was barefoot. I just got out of the car, went up to

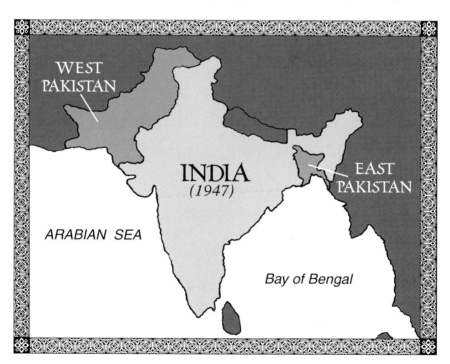

A Muslim family migrates from Hindu India to Muslim Pakistan.

the crowd and got hold of the man they were chasing and put him behind me."

The crowd asked Indira what she thought she was doing. She replied, "I am saving this man's life; you can only kill him after you have killed me." The crowd didn't recognize her and shouted that they could easily kill her too.

Indira said, "Anybody can kill me, but you are not going to, you don't have the courage and you are not going to." She said she was telling "this wretched man to run to the car and holding off the people; but he hung on to my sari [garment] and wouldn't let go, so we kept stepping backwards." The crowd finally let Indira and the man escape. After taking him to the hospital, Indira went home.

One day soon after, Gandhi called her. He had heard about what she had done, and he asked why she hadn't told him. "I didn't think it was anything special to tell you because I just acted on reflex," Indira told him. "Sometimes one has to do something without thinking. Maybe if one thought of the danger, one would hesitate, but the feeling that this has to be done is much stronger than any other thought," she continued.

In the hope of stopping the violence, Indira again volunteered to go into the troubled areas to try to negotiate a peace. It was a dangerous task, but she courageously tried to bring both Muslims and Hindus together so they could talk. Although Indira was not entirely successful, she was able to squelch some of the violence, get food to starving people, arrange for medical supplies and doctors, and help with sanitary problems.

Meanwhile, Jawaharlal was getting letters threatening Indira's safety. These letters made Jawaharlal realize the danger Indira had put herself in. He ordered police protection for her, and a military jeep with a police officer carrying a stun gun followed her around.

Finally, Indira was able to convince five Hindus and five Muslims to meet. That meeting remained peaceful, so Indira planned a tea party for five hundred people, both Muslims and Hindus. Indira made a speech, declaring that "we want peace because there is another war to fight—the war against poverty and ignorance. We have promises to keep with our people—of work, food, clothing, and shelter, health, and education."

Gandhi, now seventy-eight years old, began another fast. He refused to eat until Muslims and Hindus stopped killing each other. He would starve to death if necessary. Both Muslims and Hindus had great respect and love for Gandhi. After six days, leaders of both factions went to Gandhi and implored him to begin to take food. They told him that they would try to work our their differences. Gandhi then broke his fast.

August 15, 1947, was an important day. The British flag was lowered and the new Indian flag was raised. India was an independent country at last. Indira and all those people who had sacrificed so much for so many years finally saw the fulfillment of their dreams. India was a free country and Jawaharlal Nehru was elected its first prime minister.

"It is one of the proudest and most exciting moments in my life," Indira wrote. "It was the culmination which so many people had fought for. Yet, when it actually came, I think one was more numbed than anything. When you feel something very intensely, you can hardly feel it. You are not sure whether it has happened or not."

Jawaharlal made a famous speech, saying, "Long ago we made a tryst with destiny and now the time has come when we shall redeem our pledge. . . . It is fitting that at this solemn moment we take a pledge of dedication to the service of India and her people and to the still larger cause of humanity."

In January Indira received a letter from Gandhi, asking her to visit him. She took Rajiv with her, and they sat at Gandhi's feet and prayed and talked. Two days later, on January 30, 1948, while walking with a crowd of followers, a Hindu man assassinated Mohandas Gandhi. The killer hated Gandhi because he had tried to bring Muslims and Hindus to a peaceful settlement.

Jawaharlal Nehru is sworn in as prime minister of India by Lord Mountbatten, Great Britain's viceroy of India.

The death of Gandhi was a terrible blow to all of India. Indira and her father had come to rely on Gandhi's wise advice. No matter what they were doing for the country, it was soothing to know that Gandhi was not too far away. He had been the center around which all of India had revolved. All Indians, Hindus and Muslims, grieved his death. In her autobiography, Indira said of Gandhi, "To me Gandhi is a living man who represents the highest level to which a human being can evolve."

At Gandhi's funeral, Jawaharlal said of his dearest friend, "The light that has illumined this country these many years will illumine it for many years to come, and a thousand years later that light will still be seen in this country and in the world."

The body of Mohandas Gandi, showered with flower petals, before the funeral on February 2, 1948

During their 1949 trip to the United States, Indira and Jawaharlal visited Mount Vernon, George Washington's impressive estate in Virginia. Frances Bolton, of the House Foreign Affairs Committee, is also pictured.

 SEVEN

Sparks in the Fire

1949–1959

In April 1949, Indira made her first visit to the United States. President Harry S. Truman had invited Nehru, and Nehru asked Indira to accompany him. The U.S. government paid for the trip, and they were flown to Washington in the president's private plane. Indira liked President and Mrs. Truman.

Indira and Nehru were invited to the finest parties given by Washington's political society. However, Indira's dislike of parties and crowds prompted her to remain at the hotel while her father attended the many receptions in his honor.

The political scene also intimidated her. It was clear a few days after their arrival that their visit was arranged as an opportunity to influence Nehru. The United States wanted him to side with the West in the Cold War—an intense rivalry that developed after World War II between groups of Communist and non-Communist nations. (The struggle was called the

Cold War because it did not actually lead to wide-scale fighting.)

In 1950 India developed a policy of nonalignment, which meant it would remain neutral during the Cold War. This freedom opened the door to extensive travel for Indira and her father.

American political leaders assumed that Nehru, coming from a poor country, would be impressed with the wealth of the United States and that they could win his support with the promise of economic aid to India. Instead of Nehru and Indira being impressed with the lavishness that they witnessed, they were repulsed to find that so much money was in so few hands and that it was not shared with those who had little. The visit was a disappointment to all concerned.

In 1950, when Nehru turned sixty, he found that he needed more personal support. He lived alone in Teen Murti (which means "the House with Three Statues"), a huge English-style house with ten bedrooms and a garden. His father, wife, and teacher were all dead, so he turned to the only other person who could help him.

At first, Indira thought that she would only set up the house for her father, then return home to Feroze and pay regular visits to Nehru. But Indira soon realized that her father needed her on a daily basis. She quickly found herself in the position of hostess for many official state functions. This was a very difficult role for Indira to play because, having grown up in relative isolation, she often felt uncomfortable in the company of many people. "I used to stay for a period of time [at Teen Murti] and then go," she wrote. "Later, it became more and more difficult to leave. My husband was then working in Lucknow and I used to go there. But, invariably, I would get a telegram: 'Important guest coming, return at once.' My father would feel so hurt if I didn't come that it was very difficult to say no."

Indira was caught between the wishes of her father and her husband. Feroze didn't appreciate being deprived of his wife whenever Nehru felt he needed Indira. This tension in the marriage, and the stress of traveling back and forth between Lucknow and Delhi, was extremely taxing on Indira.

After the trip to the United States, Indira visited Indonesia at the invitation of President Sukarno. From Indonesia, Indira and Nehru traveled to Singapore and Penang, in Southeast Asia.

In 1952 Feroze was elected to the Indian National Congress as the representative from Lucknow. This enabled him to move to Delhi and be with his family. He rented a small apartment near Teen Murti but spent most of his time with Indira, who was taking a greater part in her father's political life.

Unfortunately, tension built up between Feroze and his father-in-law. Their opinions differed on almost every subject, and they found it difficult to agree on anything. Often they would start a discussion during mealtime, which often ended in a heated argument or stony silence.

In 1953 thirty-six-year-old Indira accompanied her father to Great Britain to attend the coronation of Queen Elizabeth II. There she met former prime minister Winston Churchill who had tried to block India from gaining its independence a few years before. He had also publicly said many derogatory things about Indira's family and Mohandas Gandhi. At one of the receptions, Indira found herself sitting next to Churchill. He suddenly turned to Indira and said, "Is it not strange that we should be talking as friends when we hated each other such a short while ago?" Indira replied, "But, we did not hate you." Churchill, looking away from Indira, said, "But I did, I did."

Indira also visited China and the Soviet Union in 1953 as a representative of her father. It was her first extensive travel alone. Nehru was trying to get the leaders of the world's nations to come to some sort of peaceful coexistence with each other. China had already given its support for this proposal, but many countries were against it.

Since the 1949 Communist revolution in China, Nehru had been working with the leaders of that country to find ways for the two countries—India and China—to coexist on peaceful terms. Nehru knew that once the new leadership in China was firmly established, the government would look for new territories to conquer, and he feared that China's next conquest would be India. Nehru decided to sweeten India's relationship with China.

Earlier that year, when Chinese forces entered the tiny country of Tibet, Nehru and the Indian government had openly supported the move. The Chinese did let Tibet keep its right to regional self-government and freedom of religion, however. The Dalai Lama, Tibet's religious leader, became chairman of the governing committee. Since India had supported China during the takeover of Tibet, the Chinese government agreed to sign a document called the Panchsheel Declaration, which promoted peaceful coexistence between India and China.

The United States and its allies, including Pakistan and Ceylon, condemned the declaration and instead set up their own. Nehru became angry. He and Indira had recently received unkind criticism from the United States because they were visiting Communist countries. When Nikolay Bulganin and Nikita Khrushchev, leaders of the Soviet Union, visited

Premier Zhou Enlai of China exchanges greetings with Indira.
Escott Reid, of the Canadian High Commission, looks on.

India and received a warm welcome, many U.S. leaders
feared that India was about to embrace Communism. Nehru
realized that U.S. politicians were entirely misinterpreting
these visits.

In 1955 Indira was elected to the Congress Working
Committee. Most of her work was devoted to the women's
department of the party, but this was the first small step toward her eventual political leadership.

Sometime in February 1956, Indira saw an American
newspaper article about herself. Not only were the quotes in-
accurate, but the article portrayed her and her father as new
Communists. She was very angry and upset. On February 23,
1956, Indira wrote a very emotional letter to her American
friend Dorothy Norman. Norman was a social worker,

scholar, and author who had met Indira during her 1949 visit to the United States. Indira hoped that Dorothy could use her influence with the U.S. people to correct the misunderstandings in the article.

Indira wrote her friend that "Bulganin and Khrushchev got a tremendous welcome here. There are many reasons for this but the main one was that they had accorded us a very wonderful welcome when we went to their country, and every Indian felt that we should repay their hospitality....

"All those of us who have [had] the opportunity of visiting the [C]ommunist countries are very clear in our minds that we should not follow that path and we reali[z]e that we

Jawaharlal and Indira welcome Soviet leaders Nikolay Bulganin, far right, *and Nikita Khrushchev,* second from left. *India received scrutiny from the United States because of its dealings with Communist countries.*

can only avoid this by strengthening our own organization and trying to prove to the people that ours is the better way."

Later that year, President Dwight Eisenhower invited Indira and her father to the United States. In Washington, D.C., they both attended state dinners, luncheons, and official talks and gave many interviews to the press. They traveled on to New York, where Indira spent time with Dorothy Norman.

While Nehru attended meetings, Indira and Dorothy went to the Metropolitan Museum of Art and the Museum of Modern Art. Millionaire industrialist John D. Rockefeller and his wife were very interested in Indira and invited her to their home in Tarrytown, New York. This was her first experience in an American home. However, Dorothy told Indira that the Rockefeller's home was by no means indicative of the normal American home. Most Americans lived much more simply than the Rockefellers.

At this time, Indira and Feroze were not getting along as well as Indira would have liked. The tension brought about by her duties for her father and her time spent with the children left little or no time for Feroze. Indira was getting more involved in politics than ever before. In 1956 she was elected president of the Allahabad Congress Committee, which was comparable to the office of mayor in a U.S. city. Then in 1957, Indira was elected to the Congress Central Election Committee. This committee directed the campaign for president of the Congress.

Indira traveled throughout India. She worked closely with Lal Bahadur Shastri, who was as active in the Congress as Jawaharlal and Indira. Shastri was the railway minister and was also in charge of elections. "Mr. Shastri used to take a lot of work off my father's shoulders," Indira wrote. "I worked very closely with him concerning the candidates, and he

Indira with her sons Rajiv, left, *and Sanjay,* right, *on a sightseeing trip to London in the 1950s*

would phone me wherever I was, because every day I was sent to a different place."

On her travels, Indian citizens frequently asked Indira why the United States was giving so much military aid to Pakistan, a gesture that was making Pakistan more militaristic. Pakistanis had been raiding the Indian borders, and most Indians blamed the United States for the trouble. Indira tried to sooth Indian animosities toward the United States, but her words and those of her father had little effect.

Little by little, Nehru came to depend on Indira. She was supportive of him but did not hesitate to express her opinions, even if they differed from his. Indira also corrected his behaviour from time to time. Nehru had a reputation for a quick temper in matters of politics and for an impatience with social pleasantries. He always knew by his daughter's raised eyebrows when he needed to get control of himself.

Much of the world thought Indira could sway her father in matters of state. People who felt uncomfortable taking certain issues to Nehru would lay them at the feet of his daughter, knowing that she would take them to her father. At times all this responsibility weighed heavily on Indira's shoulders.

In 1959 the Indian National Congress Party asked Indira to accept the post of president, a job her grandfather had held in 1919 and 1928. Her father had also held the position for six one-year terms. In her first presidential address to the nation, she quoted some lines from a popular Indian song: "We are the women of India./Don't imagine us as flower-maidens./We are the sparks in the fire."

In July 1959, Indira wrote a letter to Dorothy Norman, confiding that "a veritable sea of trouble is engulfing me." Indira's relationship with Feroze was disintegrating before her eyes, and she was powerless to stop it.

Indira's home was not the only troubled spot in India, however. A troubling situation was brewing in the southern state of Kerala, where the Communists were slowly taking over the government. The United States and some European countries blamed Nehru for not taking a stand against the Communists. However, he was finding that some of his ministers who were at one time anti-Communist were now supporting the takeover in Kerala.

Another situation captured Nehru's attention in 1959. In August of that year, the Chinese tightened their control of

Indira, in 1959, after being elected president of the Congress.
A portrait of Mohandas Gandhi hangs on the wall behind her in
the presidential office.

Tibet, and the Dalai Lama fled the country. The Chinese
wanted to destroy all monasteries and kill all the monks. The
new plan had been to capture the Dalai Lama and use him
to control the Tibetan people. The Tibetans asked Nehru if

the Dalai Lama could have asylum in India, and Nehru agreed without much hesitation. Indira strongly opposed the increased Chinese control of Tibet. She said, "I viewed the Tibetan problem as a human one. There were people who were being oppressed and who asked for shelter. I was not questioning China's sovereignty or anything like that, but I did feel that, when people were coming to seek refuge, it had always been India's tradition to grant it." The Dalai Lama, accompanied by hundreds of monks and nuns, secretly fled Tibet and made their home in Dharmsala, a city in northern India.

After being sworn in as president of the Congress on August 15, 1959, Indira gave a speech to the people of India. In it she said, "In mountaineering, the higher one climbs, the more hazardous the journey and the narrower and steeper the trail." She was telling Indians that gaining their independence was only the first step to becoming a strong nation. The steps would get more difficult along the way, but if they wanted to achieve the vision that she and her father had for India, it was important that they continue with courage and strength. Unfortunately, many Indian people and even some members of the Congress did not share Indira's vision.

Indira and Jawaharlal are greeted by photographers upon their 1961 arrival in the United States.

 EIGHT

In Her Father's Footsteps

1960–1964

As her presidential term came to an end, Indira took stock of her accomplishments over the past year. When she was elected, the Congress had been in debt. She helped pull it out of financial decline and made sure that money was delegated to all departments. Indira made sure that government representatives in Congress were available to the people at all times, even in the evenings and on weekends. She traveled extensively to almost every district in India and raised money to train others to conduct official business in the many districts.

Indira initiated *padyatras*, or walking engagements, during which congressional representatives walked through their districts and talked to the people. The representatives listened to the concerns of the people and then brought those concerns to the meetings of the Congress.

There was one area, however, where Indira felt that her efforts were unsuccessful. She tried to restructure the

Congress Party, but she was not influential enough to make any significant changes.

In the spring of 1960, forty-three-year-old Indira was asked to run for a second term as president of the Congress, but she declined. Nehru was almost seventy years old, and the burden of his responsibilities was becoming greater with each passing year. Indira found her roles of mother, wife, and assistant to her father taxing. Those responsibilities, combined with the extensive travel and pressure associated with the position of president of the Congress, was more than she could handle at this time.

Indira and Feroze decided to take a second honeymoon. They spent a month in beautiful Kashmir in northern India. Feroze had suffered a heart attack earlier in the year, and Indira tried to nurse him back to health. It took a serious illness to bring their marriage together again.

Soon after the couple returned from Kashmir, Indira flew to Kerala, a region that Communists had recently taken over. Kerala was having severe problems due to a food shortage and race riots agitated by the Communist Party. On July 21, 1959, Indira wrote Dorothy Norman about the situation in Kerala:

> The Kerala situation is worsening. This movement is not petering out as the Communists claim but gathering momentum. The women, whom I have been trying to organize for years, had always refused to come into politics. Now they are out in the field. Over eight thousand have been arrested. I have heard that in Europe and perhaps in America my father is being blamed for not taking any action. He has given a very good lead from the beginning but he is incapable of dictatorship or roughshodding over the views of his senior colleagues. More and

> more I find that he is almost the only one who thinks
> in terms of ideology rather than personality. I cannot
> write much in a letter but you would be surprised
> that some of the ministers whom we had considered
> the most anti-Communist are now supporting the
> Communist government of Kerala.

On the flight home to Delhi, Indira reviewed her visit. She decided that although her visit wasn't totally successful in solving all of Kerala's problems, her presence there had been helpful.

When Indira's plane landed at the Delhi airport, she was quickly ushered into a waiting car and driven to the hospital. Feroze had had another heart attack. She stayed by his side all night, until he died in the early morning of September 8, 1960. Indira was heartbroken. Although their marriage had not been as intimate as she would have liked, she had loved Feroze. Indira tried to carry on her responsibilities despite her grief.

Since both her children were in school, she found more time for travel commitments. In 1961 she accepted an invitation from President John F. Kennedy to visit the United States and meet with him.

After Indira left Washington, Lady Bird Johnson, the wife of the vice president, told reporters, "To see India, you must visit the villages. To understand India you must read Tagore. But to know India you must have a teacher like Indira Gandhi. I was lucky because I had all three."

In October 1962, the Chinese attacked India. Although Nehru had tried to remain on friendly terms with the Chinese, China was angry that India was providing sanctuary to the Dalai Lama and his followers. During the fighting, Indira made several trips to the front. She went without the permission of

President John F. Kennedy and First Lady Jacqueline Kennedy greet Indira and Jawaharlal before a private dinner at the White House.

her father or other members of the government. It was dangerous, and the army did not want her there, but the people in Gauhati, Tezpur, and other northeastern cities near the fighting were happy to see Indira.

China demanded sixteen thousand square miles of Indian land along the Chinese border. Nehru refused to negotiate. He sent the Indian army to defend the border, but it was badly defeated by the Chinese. Within a month, a cease-fire was called, and India handed over the land. The land was worthless, but China had demonstrated its power over the Indian government.

India's defeat was a devastating blow to Nehru. His health began to deteriorate, and Indira found herself doing much of his work. In addition to doing much of the paperwork required by a person in Nehru's position, Indira traveled, both alone and with her father. She made frequent trips to the United States and to Paris during 1962 and 1963.

The stress from Indira's political life was taking its toll on her body. She suffered from frequent infections, fatigue, and depression. No matter where she went, hordes of people followed her, asking for favors. She had not a moment's peace for her own thoughts. In October 1963, Indira began to plan for her future. She had seen a little house in London that she desperately wanted to buy. She felt that her father, Rajiv, and Sanjay had kept her in Delhi, but now that Rajiv was in school in England and Sanjay was about to join him, she would be free to live there too. While she was working out her finances, however, someone else bought the house. Indira was devastated but remained determined to fulfill her dream.

Six months later, in May 1964, her father died from a stroke at the age of seventy-four. In writing about her father's death, Indira said, "Personal grief is so minute a part of the void which he has left. He burnt with a 'gemlike flame.' How can I believe that it can go out? I feel his presence all round and pray that it may always be so."

After Nehru's death, many people assumed that Indira would take over as acting prime minister until the next election. Indira, however, did not plan to do so. She was exhausted—mentally, emotionally, and physically. She tried to gently bow out of politics, but that didn't seem to be her destiny.

Lal Bahadur Shastri served as prime minister until the next election. He asked Indira to accept the ministerial position of Minister of Information and Broadcasting. Shastri thought having Indira in his cabinet would increase the popularity of his administration. Indira was reluctant to take on such an important position because she had been under an enormous strain following her father's death. Once she learned that the Indian government was planning an exhibition of her father's life in New York, however, she accepted the position.

On May 28, 1964, millions of people gathered at the funeral pyre of Prime Minister Nehru to mourn his death.

It was difficult to follow in the footsteps of Prime Minister Jawaharlal Nehru. Most Indians had loved him and viewed him as their savior. They saw Mr. Shastri as an indecisive leader, which made the people uneasy. Then in August 1965, Pakistan invaded India.

Indira at an Indian Embassy reception shortly after first becoming prime minister in 1966. (The other people are not identified.)

 NINE

Lady Prime Minister

1965–1971

Muslim leaders in Pakistan had never really accepted the division of territory that Nehru had decided upon in the 1940s. They thought that by launching a surprise attack, they could disarm the Indian government and capture Kashmir. But they hadn't counted on the speed with which the Indian army was able to retaliate.

Indira had just landed in Kashmir for a short vacation with Sanjay, when she heard about the Pakistani invasion. As she disembarked from the plane, she saw the entire cabinet "looking white as sheets." They told her that Pakistan had invaded Kashmir, and a band of rebels was heading for the airport. "If you don't do something quickly you can't save us," they told her. The cabinet escorted Indira to a meeting in Srinagar, the capital of Kashmir. Cabinet members told her that there was a major infiltration of Pakistani rebels in Kashmir, and they felt that fighting would be imminent. Indira phoned Delhi, requesting troops be sent to Srinagar.

At about one in the morning, Indira and the other cabinet members could hear firing on the outskirts of Srinagar. Indira then assumed her role as Minister of Information and Broadcasting. Indira went on the radio and talked to the people about keeping up morale. She underplayed the strength of the Pakistani forces. She then convinced the director of Radio Kashmir to drive her through parts of Srinagar so she could assess for herself the conditions in these dangerous areas. She reported regularly to Mr. Shastri to prepare him for the possibility that this skirmish could escalate into a major war. Four weeks later, Indira's prophecy came true. Pakistani

As part of a national campaign, women in Dhaka, Pakistan, practice rifle shooting in 1965. The brewing conflict between India and Pakistan over the region of Kashmir prompted these actions.

planes dropped bombs on India as troops and tanks attacked from the west. Indira set up a citizens' committee to keep up the morale of the people. She also reported conditions to Mr. Shastri, who ordered the Indian forces to attack Pakistan, thereby ending the brief war. Pakistan's plan to annex Kashmir had failed.

When Mr. Shastri died shortly thereafter, on January 10, 1966, many members of the Congress Party hoped Indira would become prime minister. Indira was running against Morarji Desai, a man who was opposed to almost everything that she and her father had stood for. When elections were held, Indira won by a wide margin: 355 parliamentary votes for Indira and 169 for Desai.

As Indira left the Parliament building after the election, crowds gathered to celebrate her victory. Women members of Parliament showered her with rose petals, and one of them pinned a red rosebud on Indira's shawl—just like the one her father had always worn in the buttonhole of his jacket. Security men had to link arms to prevent Indira from being knocked over by the crowds. Early the next day, Indira visited the cremation shrines of Mohandas Gandhi and her father. She placed offerings there, as was the Hindu custom, and recited prayers.

On January 24, 1966, Indira was sworn in as India's third prime minister—and its first woman prime minister. Dressed in a white sari, Indira took the oath of office. Later that day, her inaugural address was broadcast over All India Radio.

She talked about her plans to increase agricultural production with modern methods of farming. Greater food production meant greater self-reliance. Indira wanted to build up India, to give jobs to the poor so they could take part in the economic development of their country and carn enough to

Indira, pictured here in New Delhi, was elected prime minister of India on January 19, 1966. Members of Parliament elected Indira by secret ballots.

feed their families. She talked about the peace and friendship that India was intent on developing with all nations but added that "we must be alert and keep constant vigil, strengthening our defenses as necessary." Indira spoke of the goals and dreams that her father and Shastri had held and worked for, and she promised to uphold those same ideals.

Shortly after Indira had been sworn in as prime minister, President Lyndon Johnson invited her to visit the United States. This would be her fourth trip to the United States since 1960. But before she could think of leaving the country, Indira had to deal with certain problems in India.

There had been a major drought in Kerala, Orissa, and other areas of India. Indira ordered food to be rushed to these areas and instituted a program whereby grains would be imported, particularly from the United States. She also persuaded state governments to take part in relief work and plans for food distribution.

At this same time, Sikhs were demanding a separate state where the official language would be Punjabi. The Sikhs, who live primarily in northern India, are a religious group of about fourteen million. The British dissolved the Sikhs' autonomy in the nineteenth century, and they had been fighting for a separate state since then.

The issue arose again in 1966. Indira's government agreed to make Punjabi—rather than Hindi—the official language of the Punjab region. Then to appease the conservative Hindu population in the Punjab region, Indira established a separate Hindu state called Haryana.

Indians from the drought-ridden village of Vaini create an irrigation ditch to direct water to their crops. Drought and famine were common throughout India in the early 1960s.

Indira's next challenge was the economic stability of the country. She proposed a new economic program and, on the advice of the experts in the finance ministry, devalued the rupee—India's basic unit of money—by 36 percent in an effort to improve India's foreign exchange situation. Indira knew little about economics, so she depended on these experts to provide her with intelligent advice. Eventually, she realized that devaluing the currency was a mistake that caused even greater economic problems, but she did demonstrate that she was not afraid to make bold decisions.

When Indira finally did get to Washington, the president and Mrs. Johnson gave her a warm reception. Indira soon became angry and frustrated with the president, however. India had been pleading with the United States for a shipment of wheat. President Lyndon Johnson kept delaying the shipment and when asked, his advisers said that " the papers were on the president's desk." If she had known that a wheat shipment hadn't been scheduled for India, she could have instituted stricter rationing. Now, many people would suffer hunger while India waited for help from the United States.

Soon after Indira returned to Delhi, she began a series of trips throughout India. Crowds of people continually surrounded and followed her, no matter what time of day or how hot the temperatures. Indira had to show her "political face" continuously, waving and talking to people. Only when she returned to her rooms could she relax.

After leaving Mumbai, Indira traveled to Poona, an area that had been hit particularly hard by drought and famine. Here, with temperatures reaching 110 degrees Fahrenheit in the early morning, the crowds still followed her. Indira spent the morning attending meetings, reviewing irrigation plans with the officials, and trying to raise the morale of the citizens.

President Lyndon Johnson and First Lady Lady Bird Johnson present Indira with a bouquet of roses during her 1966 visit.

In the afternoon, she visited the military hospitals and rehabilitation centers for the veterans of the Indian army, and in the evening she attended a reception in her honor. The next day, Indira flew to Mahabaleshwar to see an army training program, then back to Poona, and then home to Delhi.

Weary and emotionally exhausted from her travels, Indira wrote to her friend Dorothy in February 1967: "Ever since plastic surgery was heard of, I have been wanting to get something done to my nose. I even started by putting by money for it and I thought the only way it could be done without the usual hoo-ha was first to have some slight accident which would enable me to have it put right."

Her wish was soon fulfilled. Indira was speaking in Bhubaneswar, on the west coast of India, when some student agitators started to throw pebbles. After her speech, officials

Despite a broken nose, Indira fulfilled every one of her speaking engagements. She is pictured here in New Delhi, February 16, 1967, with Sarvepalli Radhakrishnan, president of India.

suggested that Indira sit at the back of the stage so she wouldn't be hurt by the agitators. Instead, she insisted that she remain in the front of the dais, since she was the guest speaker. Suddenly, Indira was thrown from her seat. Someone had thrown a brick and hit her in the nose. Blood spurted from her face and Indira thought her nose was broken. When she looked in the mirror, she saw that her nose was crooked.

She later wrote, "As it was I tried to put it right myself and heard a little 'tik' sound. The left lip had swollen to the size of a big egg. Most of my face was also discoloured and I bled for quite a while through the nose."

Indira was not one to be stilled by a broken nose. With a huge bandage on her face, she fulfilled her other speaking engagements for the next three days. Only then did she go to Willingdon Hospital and have her broken nose set.

Elections were scheduled for March 1967. Indira continued traveling throughout India, covering an area of more than 15,000 miles and making 160 public speeches. On March 12, 1967, fifty-year-old Indira was elected prime minister—this time by the Indian people.

In September 1967, Indira traveled to Russia, Poland, Yugoslavia (then made up of the republics of Serbia, Montenegro, Bosnia-Herzegovina, Croatia, Macedonia, and Slovenia), Romania, and Bulgaria. She also established a ministry for atomic energy to plan for making an atomic bomb.

China had a very active nuclear program, and Indira was afraid that if India did not keep up, the country would be considered weak and open to attack. After the invasion, China had made threats to India.

In 1969 Indira's son Rajiv was married. His wife, Sonia, an Italian woman, was described by Indira as "beautiful, . . . a really nice girl, wholesome and straightforward." At the time, Rajiv was a pilot for Air India.

In a December 17, 1970, radio address, Indira announced that elections were to be scheduled for February 1971. She was at the height of her popularity, and this seemed to be good time to run for reelection. Morarji Desai, an ambitious, outspoken leader, led the opposition party, called the Syndicate. Desai used the motto Indira Hatao (Remove Indira);

Indira countered with her own motto, Garibi Hatao (Remove Poverty). Indians responded to Indira and the promise she was making. Most Indians were extremely poor, and they believed they had found their savior in Indira.

Indira ran her election campaign almost single-handedly. She whirled through India with an exciting energy and ferociousness. Sometimes she stood in an open space for hours at a time so people could see her easily. She used words and expressions that appealed to the masses and their specific problems in different regions of the country.

After an overwhelming victory, Indira is sworn in for a second term in 1971. (The other people are not identified.)

The election resulted in an overwhelming victory for Indira. The Congress won 352 seats, and the opposing party almost dissolved. On March 1, 1971, Prime Minister Indira Gandhi was sworn in for a second term.

Indira, speaking with the press here, faced many challenges in her second term as prime minister.

 TEN

Clouds over India

1972–1979

In 1971 civil war broke out between East Pakistan and West Pakistan. The trouble began when the representative from East Pakistan won a majority of votes in an election. The West Pakistanis, the majority of them being from a higher Indian caste, refused to be ruled by an East Pakistani.

Indira was hesitant to become involved in the war, for several reasons. First of all, China was one of Pakistan's allies, and India did not want to get into a conflict with China. China would have loved to use India's involvement in Pakistan's civil war as an excuse to invade India. Also, the United States supported West Pakistan. However, when Indira learned that thousands of Indians had already been killed and millions of refugees were streaming into the Indian state of Bengal on the eastern border, she realized that she had to take a stand.

Indira traveled to Moscow and met with Soviet leader Leonid Brezhnev to sign a peace treaty. Then she visited England, France, Germany, and Austria, asking for financial and food assistance for the refugees fleeing from Pakistan.

On December 3, 1971, the Pakistani air force bombed eight Indian air fields. This action forced Indira to declare war on Pakistan. She sent the army into East Pakistan. In response, the United States sent arms to East Pakistan, and a fleet of U.S. naval battle ships moved into the Bay of Bengal with the intention of forcing India to call back its troops. Meanwhile, the Soviet Union came to India's aid. Brezhnev sent Soviet ships into the Bay of Bengal and announced to both the United States and China that the Soviet Union was willing to defend India from any aggression from either country. With the support of the Soviet Union, India continued to move into East Pakistan.

Newspapers in the United States condemned India as an aggressive nation. Indira was angered and hurt by these accusations and the continued lack of support from the United States. Indira wrote an impassioned letter to U.S. president Richard Nixon. She told him that she felt it was unfair of the United States to blame India for the strife in her country. She told him that India had done all it could to avert war, and that it would have been more successful had the United States and other major nations of the world supported India in its efforts. On December 14, the Pakistanis surrendered. In the peace agreement, Indira gave East Pakistan its freedom and declared it an independent nation, renamed Bangladesh.

The Pakistani war was only the start of India's problems over the next three years. Poverty and hunger plagued India with a severity unknown in recent years. India had incurred a huge debt while borrowing from other countries to help its impoverished citizens. Indira tried to limit imported goods into the country, thinking that more cottage industries would spring up, but the people were tired—tired of war, of disease,

Troops from the Indian army patrol the border between India and East Pakistan in 1971.

of poverty. Workers, dissatisfied with working conditions and poverty-level pay, crippled India with thousands of strikes.

In April 1974, the railway workers went on strike, stopping transportation of food, goods, and people throughout India. Indira reacted by having the strikers and union leaders arrested. Some members of the police got violent with the strikers and even set fire to their homes. These actions made Indira unpopular with many Indian factions.

In India, refugees board a truck to return to their homes in the newly formed country of Bangladesh.

On May 18, 1974, Indira took a step toward joining the nuclear race. India exploded an underground nuclear device, thus becoming the world's sixth nuclear power. Indira wanted to develop nuclear devices for two major reasons. She thought nuclear energy could provide inexpensive electrical power to the country, and she saw atomic energy being used in many fields, such as medicine. However, the major nations of the world were deeply concerned about another nation gaining access to nuclear power.

The dissatisfaction and unrest on the part of the Indian people intensified as India's many problems grew worse. As a result, Indira declared a state of emergency on June 26, 1975. This meant that the government had the liberty to impose heavy restrictions on its citizens. General elections were cancelled; thousands of opposition leaders, students, journalists, and lawyers were arrested and imprisoned without a trial; and the government censored newspapers and radio.

In a country whose people had fought so hard and so long for their freedom, these restrictions were thought to be in direct opposition to the democratic philosophy that Indira's father and grandfather had worked for. Many Indians feared that Indira's government had become a dictatorship and that all their freedoms would again be taken away.

Citizens in the United States were outraged at the apparent dictatorial tactics Indira and her government had imposed. As harsh as the measures seemed to the Indian nation and to the rest of the world, the state of emergency did have some beneficial results. India's agricultural and industrial production and exports rose to a new high. Many of India's cities were cleaned up, stricter laws regarding smuggling were enacted and enforced, beggars were taken off the streets and given shelter and food, and discipline was reestablished throughout the country.

At this time, Indira's son Sanjay began to take an active role in Indian politics. He became a staunch supporter of his mother's politics and frequently advised her during India's state of emergency. Sanjay, who had not been successful in any other endeavor he had attempted, including graduating from college, decided that he could leave his mark in the political arena.

Sanjay instituted a five-point program for social reform to clean up the cities and reforest India's land. He wanted to end the caste system and the custom of dowries, whereby a woman's family had to pay the husband money before the couple could marry. He also wanted to enact a system of birth control to stop the ever increasing birthrate in the country. According to numerous reports, however, Sanjay's methods of carrying out certain parts of the program were ruthless and inhumane.

One aspect of Sanjay's social reform program was to clean up the cities by building new housing. But first the old, dilapidated houses had to be removed. Reports circulated that Sanjay ordered the burning of entire Muslim neighborhoods in Delhi. When a group of Muslims tried to defend their homes, the police fired into the crowds, killing several people.

Sanjay then proposed that India's population be controlled by the government. There were more than 700 million people in India. Too many people for one nation to feed, clothe, and shelter. Sanjay believed that forced sterilization was the only way to control the birthrate. It was reported that he ordered the police to accompany doctors and medical teams to scour the countryside in vans, forcing people to undergo a sterilization operation, with or without their consent.

Indira fully supported her son's plans for reform, but it is unclear whether she knew what methods he was using to expedite them. Although Sanjay had no formal position in government, he acted on the authority of his mother. Indira told critics, "Those who attack Sanjay attack me." Indira's popularity had taken a serious dive because of her emergency act, but her support of Sanjay's actions made her even more unpopular. In March 1977, against the advice of her son, Indira lifted the state of emergency. She released from prison the

Sanjay, front left in the car, *toured the country to increase support for his mother's economic reform program. He is pictured here in Kolkata in 1976.*

hundred thousand or so of her enemies. She then called for elections to take place. Indira was defeated after eleven years as prime minister.

One of the fortunate aspects of losing the election was that after so many years, Indira was able to relax and enjoy her family. Rajiv and Sonia had given her two grandchildren, for whom she rarely had time over the years. As a private citizen, she spent her days in her garden and playing with her grandchildren. She decided to hold *durbar* (private interviews) as she had when her father was prime minister. A steady stream of visitors complained about the new government.

A crowd gathers in New Delhi to celebrate Indira Gandhi's birthday on November 19, 1979.

In November 1978, Indira was elected to Parliament. The government was so afraid that she would regain her popularity that they had Indira and Sanjay arrested. After a week in jail, they were released, but her seat in Parliament had been taken away from her.

In 1979 opposition leaders proposed that a court be set up to try Indira, Sanjay, and the government for certain actions taken during the state of emergency. This never took place, however.

Indira, pictured here in 1981, was elected prime minister for a third term on January 3, 1980.

 ELEVEN

A Sad Day for India

1980–1984

In December 1979, new elections were held, and on January 3, 1980, Indira Gandhi, then sixty-two years old, was sworn in as prime minister for a third term. Indira and Sanjay worked as a team. She wrote down her thoughts and compared them to Sanjay's ideas. Indira looked to Sanjay for support and advice. Then suddenly on June 23, 1980, Sanjay was killed. The small plane he was flying crashed into a field in Delhi.

People had mixed feelings regarding Sanjay's death. Many women who understood what it was like to lose a child sympathized with Indira's grief. However, some people remembered the inhumane sterilization campaigns Sanjay had led, and the Muslim community recalled the homes they had lost during Sanjay's reign of terror. They felt that his death was a relief.

Indira found the grief overwhelming. She had lost not only a son, but a friend and adviser. Indira had also lost a possible heir to the prime ministership. Although the Indian people most likely would never have voted for Sanjay, most Indians couldn't conceive of a prime minister who wasn't a Nehru. So Indira and India looked to Rajiv to follow his mother in government.

Rajiv, up to this time, had deliberately stayed out of politics. He was not interested in getting involved in the intricacies of government. He was a pilot for Air India and had a comfortable life with his wife and two sons. But Indira pleaded with him to take Sanjay's place—to govern India with her and be at her side.

Indira with Sanjay in Delhi, just before he died in a plane crash

Maneka Gandhi, Sanjay's widow, formed her own political party after his death. The twenty-six year-old was seeking Sanjay's vacant parliamentary seat.

Meanwhile, Sanjay's widow, Maneka, announced that she would like to take her husband's seat in Parliament. The people felt that she was even more radical than her husband. She became very angry when the seat was eventually given to Rajiv in June 1981. In her anger, Maneka formed her own party called the National Sanjay Organization. This party was in direct opposition to the ideas that Rajiv and Indira stood for. Maneka hoped to unseat Rajiv in the next election. Rajiv, unlike his brother, was creating a following for himself with intelligence rather than force. A softspoken man, he tried to entice young people who were dedicated to the welfare of India rather than their own greed.

In her third term, Indira had to deal with the Sikhs once again. In the early 1980s, a militant group of Sikhs gained

Indian army troops on the lookout just blocks from the rebel Sikhs' hideout in the Golden Temple

greater power in Punjab and demanded that a separate state called Khalistan be created. These Sikh rebels used terrorist tactics to achieve their goals. The leader of the group, Sant Jarnail Singh Bhindranwale, openly opposed the Indian government and sent his men around the country murdering people to demonstrate his power.

On June 5, 1984, Bhindranwale and his men were hiding in the Golden Temple, the main temple of the Sikhs, located in the sacred city of Amritsar in Punjab. Indira ordered the Indian army to storm the temple and flush them out. Bhindranwale and hundreds of his men were killed. The Sikh community then had a reason to make him a martyred hero, and the militant Sikh movement grew even stronger.

On the morning of October 31, 1984, Indira was going to her office from the cottage where she lived. The two buildings were across the yard from each other, and her two Sikh bodyguards were standing at the gate. Since the problem with the Sikhs had erupted, Rajiv was uncomfortable with having Sikhs as bodyguards, but Indira was not bothered by it. Hadn't they guarded her for nine years?

Indira was excited that morning. She was dressed impeccably, as always, but that day she wore a saffron-colored sari and had taken off the bulletproof vest that Rajiv had encouraged her to wear lately. She wanted to look her best because she was going to be interviewed by the famous British actor and playwright Peter Ustinov. As Indira approached the gate leading to her office, the two guards opened fire on Indira, killing her instantly. They then continued to empty their machine guns into her body.

Peter Ustinov, who was waiting for her in the prime minister's office, heard the shots and described the scene: "We were ready with the mike and the camera. A secretary had gone to fetch her, and then it happened. I heard three single shots. We looked alarmed, but the people in the office said it must be firecrackers. Then there was a burst of automatic fire as if the attackers were making sure of it. I didn't think she had a chance. . . . We saw soldiers running. They kept us there for five hours. It became like a prison."

The entire nation was in shock over the news of Indira's death. Hindus, upon hearing about the Sikh assassins, started attacking Sikhs in the streets, burning their homes, and slaughtering their children. Rajiv was sworn in as prime minister a few hours after his mother's death. He begged Hindus to stop their violence. He told them that his mother would never have approved of their actions. Rajiv set up safe

After the news of Indira's assassination spread, riots broke out across New Delhi, causing numerous fires.

camps for Sikh families and ordered the army and police to protect them.

Once the violence was abated, India turned its emotions to grief. The loss of their beloved Indira was a deep sorrow. She had not been able to achieve everything she had wanted for India, but Indians knew that she had tried her hardest. They loved her because they knew that she had always loved India.

Indira may have suspected that she might not live much longer. Two days before her death, while giving a talk in the state of Orissa, one member of the audience asked about the many threats that had recently been made on her life. In reply, Indira said, "Such things do not worry me. When I die every single drop of my blood will invigorate the nation and strengthen united India."

An entire nation mourned after Indira Gandhi's assassination. Her body was carried through the streets of New Delhi in a funeral procession.

CHRONOLOGY

Nov. 19, 1917	Born Indira Priyadashini Nehru in Prayagraj (then Allahabad), India
1929	Organizes children's political organization, the "Monkey Brigade"
Feb. 28, 1936	Mother, Kamala Nehru, dies of tuberculosis
March 26, 1942	Marries Feroze Gandhi
Sept. 1942	Imprisoned by British for supporting Indian civil disobedience
Aug. 20, 1944	Gives birth to son Rajiv
Dec. 14, 1946	Gives birth to son Sanjay
Aug. 14, 1947	India achieves independence from Britian; Indira's father, Jawaharlal Nehru, becomes the nation's first prime minister
Jan. 30, 1948	Mohandas Gandhi assassinated by Hindu extremist
1955	Indira elected to the Congress Working Committee
1956	Elected president of the Allahabad Congress Committee
1957	Elected to the Congress Central Election Committee
Feb. 1959	President of the National Congress Party
Aug. 15, 1959	Becomes president of Indian Congress
Sept. 8, 1960	Feroze Gandhi dies
1961 & 1962	Indira visits the United States and Paris

Oct. 20, 1962	China invades India and annexes border territory
1964	Indira visits the United States and the Soviet Union
May 26, 1964	Nehru dies
Aug.-Dec. 1965	Indo-Pakistani War takes place
Jan 19, 1966	Indira elected prime minister of India by Parliament
March 12, 1967	Elected prime minister by the Indian people
Sept 1967	Travels to former Soviet Union; establishes a ministry for atomic energy
Feb. 1971	Indira reelected prime minister
Dec. 1971	War with Pakistan; East Pakistan becomes Bangladesh
June 12, 1975	Indira found guilty of electoral fraud; asked to resign
June 26, 1975	Declares state of emergency due to political unrest
March 1977	State of emergency ended; Indira defeated in election
Nov. 1978	Indira elected to Parliament
Jan. 3, 1980	Elected prime minister for the third time
June. 23, 1980	Sanjay dies in plane crash
Oct. 31, 1984	Indira Gandhi assassinated by Sikh extremists

THE RELIGIONS OF INDIA

Religion has an important role in the lives of most Indians, but the country has no official religion. About 80 percent of the Indian people are Hindus, and about 12 percent are Muslims. Smaller percentages of people practice other religions.

Christianity is the religion based on the life and teachings of Jesus Christ. Most followers of Christianity, called Christians, are members of one of three major groups: Roman Catholic, Protestant, or Eastern Orthodox. These groups have different beliefs about Jesus and his teachings, but all consider Jesus central to their religion. Christians believe that there is one God, who created the universe and continues to care for it. Christianity teaches that God sent his son, Jesus, to help people fulfill their religious duties. Roman Catholic, Eastern Orthodox, and many Protestant churches accept the doctrine of the Trinity—the belief that in one God there are three persons, the Father, the Son, and the Holy Spirit. Christianity spread in India after the Europeans arrived. Indian Christians live mainly in the southern states of Kerala and Tamil Nadu and in the tribal regions of northeastern India.

Hinduism is based on many sacred texts including the Vedas, the Upanishads, and the Puranas. Hindus believe in reincarnation—a belief that only a person's body dies, and the soul is reborn in another body. When a person achieves spiritual perfection, the soul enters a higher state of existence. Hinduism teaches *ahimsa* (nonviolence), *yoga* (a spiritual discipline involving fitness of body and mind), and the unimportance of material goods. Hindus consider cows to be sacred and, therefore, do not eat beef. People who follow Hinduism also believe in a single spiritual force—God, also called Brahman—that takes many forms. These forms make up the many gods and goddesses of the Hindu religion.

Islam came to India in the A.D. 700s, but most Indian Muslims are descendants of converted Hindus. Islam is the religion taught by the prophet Muhammad in the A.D. 600s. The term *Islam* means "surrender" or "submission." God is called Allah. A person who follows the teaching of Islam is called a Muslim. The Quran (sometimes spelled Koran) is the holy book of the Muslims, who believe it contains God's actual words. Islamic law is based on the Quran and the *sunna* (SOON-uh), the words and practices of Muhammad. Islam is the world's second largest religion. Devout Muslims are required to pray five times a day, and prayer—called *salat* (suh-LAHT)—is a Muslim's most important demonstration of devotion to God.

Jainism was founded in India in the 500s B.C. by a religious reformer named Mahavira. Jains believe that all life is sacred, and most are strict vegetarians.

Judaism is the world's oldest major religion and the first to teach the belief in one God—a God who wants people to do what is just and merciful. The basic laws and teachings of Judaism come from the Torah, the first five books of the Hebrew Bible. The Hebrew Bible is what Christians call the Old Testament. Judaism instructs people to serve God by studying the scriptures and practicing what they teach. These teachings include both ritual practices and ethical laws. Judaism holds the belief that all people are created in the image of God and deserve to be treated with dignity and respect. India has had a Jewish community since about the A.D. 100s, but many Indian Jews moved to Israel during the 1950s and 1960s.

Sikhism is a religion founded in India by Nanak, a guru (religious teacher) who lived in the late 1400s and early 1500s. Sikhs take pride in their bravery and do not believe in the caste system. Many Sikh men use the same last name, Singh (which means "lion") as a symbol of equality. Sikhs make up a large part of the Indian army.

Zoroastrianism (zawr-oh-AS-tree-uh-nihz-uhm) is a religion founded between 1400 and 1000 B.C. by a Persian prophet named Zoroaster. The religion teaches a belief in one god, Ahura Mazda, who created all things. At the heart of Zoroastrianism is the belief in a battle between good and evil. At the end of worldly time, after their bodies have been resurrected, everyone will be judged by Ahura Mazda according to how well they fought for good. India has the largest population of Zoroastrians in the world. In India, followers are called Parsis.

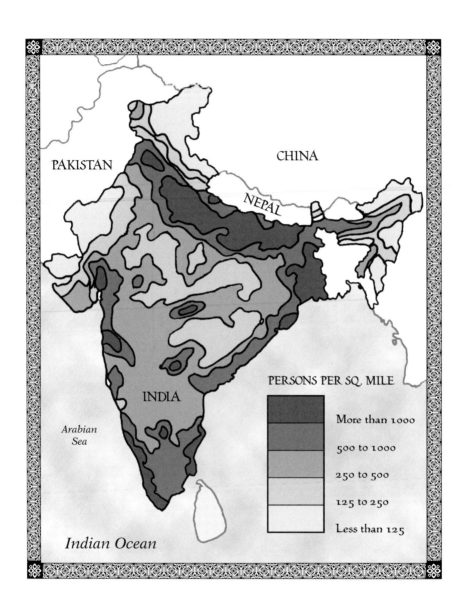

PAKISTAN

CHINA

NEPAL

INDIA

Arabian
Sea

Indian Ocean

PERSONS PER SQ. MILE

More than 1000

500 to 1000

250 to 500

125 to 250

Less than 125

120

Sources

p. 17   Francella Butler, *Indira Gandhi* (New York: Chelsea House, 1986), 19.

p. 22   Indira Gandhi, *My Truth* (New York: Grove Press, 1980), 16–17.

p. 27   Ibid., 13.

p. 34   Ibid., 23.

p. 35   Jawaharlal Nehru, *Glimpses of World History* (New York: The John Day Co., 1942), 95.

p. 43   *My Truth*, 26.

p. 47   Ibid., 44–45.

p. 54   Ibid., 53.

p. 55   Ibid., 54.

p. 61   Ibid., 60.

p. 62   Ibid.

p. 62   Ibid.

p. 63   Ibid., 63.

p. 63   Ibid., 58.

p. 63   Ibid.

p. 65   Ibid., 65.

p. 65   Ibid.

p. 68   Ibid., 69–70.

p. 69   Krishan Bhatia, *Indira: A Biography of Prime Minister Gandhi* (New York: Praeger Publishers, 1974), 139.

p. 72   Dorothy Norman, *Indira Gandhi: Letters to an American Friend* (New York: Harcourt Brace Jovanovich, 1985), 30.

p. 73   *My Truth*, 81.

p. 75   *Indira Gandhi: Letters to an American Friend*, 57.

p. 77   *My Truth*, 91.

p. 77   Ibid., 85.

p. 81   *Indira Gandhi: Letters to an American Friend*, 57.

p. 81   *My Truth*, 113.

p. 83   *Indira Gandhi: Letters to an American Friend*, 83.

p. 87   *My Truth*, 106.

p. 90   Christman, Henry M., ed. *Indira Gandhi Speaks: On Democracy, Socialism, and Third World Nonalignment* (New York: Taplinger Publishing Company, 1973), 22.

p. 93   *Indira Gandhi: Letters to an American Friend*, 117.

p. 95   Ibid., 117–118.

p. 95   Ibid., 125.

p. 104   *Indira Gandhi*, Butler, 94.

p. 113   Inder Malhotra, *Indira Gandhi: A Personal and Political Biography* (Boston: Northeastern University Press, 1991), 17.

p. 115   *Indira Gandhi: Letters to an American Friend*, 179.

Bibliography

Bhatia, Krishan. *Indira: A Biography of Prime Minister Gandhi.* New York: Praeger Publishers, 1974.

Butler, Francella. *Indira Gandhi.* New York: Chelsea House, 1986.

Christman, Henry M., ed. *Indira Gandhi Speaks: On Democracy, Socialism, and Third World Nonalignment.* New York: Taplinger Publishing Company, 1973.

Currimbhoy, Nayana. *Indira Gandhi.* New York: Franklin Watts, 1985.

Gandhi, Indira. *My Truth.* New York: Grove Press, 1980.

Gandhi, Mohandas K. *Gandhi: An Autobiography.* reprint, Boston: Beacon Press, 1961.

Garnett, Emmeline. *Madame Prime Minister: The Story of Indira Gandhi.* New York: Farrar, Straus & Giroux, 1967.

Malhotra, Inder. *Indira Gandhi: A Personal and Political Biography.* Boston: Northeastern University Press, 1991.

Nehru, Jawaharlal. *Glimpses of World History.* New York: The John Day Co., 1942.

_____. *Toward Freedom.* New York: The John Day Co., 1941.

Norman, Dorothy. *Indira Gandhi: Letters to an American Friend.* New York: Harcourt Brace Jovanovich, 1985.

Sahgal, Nayantara. *Indira Gandhi: Her Road to Power.* New York: Frederick Ungar Publishing Co., 1978.

Tagore, Rabindranath. *Collected Poems and Plays of Rabindranath Tagore.* New York: Macmillan Co., 1937.

For Further Reading

Butler, Francella. *Indira Gandhi.* New York: Chelsea House, 1986.

Church, Carol B., Gary E. McCuen, and David L. Bender, eds. *Indira Gandhi: Rose of India.* San Diego: Greenhaven Press, 1976.

Frank, Katherine. *Indira Gandhi.* New York: Houghton Mifflin Co., 2001.

Gandhi, Mohandas. *All Men Are Brothers: The Life and Thoughts of Mahatma Gandhi As Told in His Own Words.* reprint New York: Greenleaf Books, 1982.

_____ *Gandhi: An Autobiography: The Story of My Experience With Truth.* reprint, Boston: Beacon Press, 1993.

Gibson, Michael. *Gandhi and Nehru.* East Sussex, England: Wayland, 1981.

Greene, Carol. *Indira Nehru Gandhi, Ruler of India.* Chicago: Childrens Press, 1985.

Jayakar, Pupul. *Indira Gandhi: An Intimate Biography.* New York: Pantheon Books, 1993.

Martin, Christopher. *Mohandas Gandhi.* Minneapolis: Lerner Publications Co., 2001.

Mitchell, Pratima. *Gandhi: The Father of Modern India.* New York: Oxford University Press, 1998.

Rawding, F. W. *Gandhi and the Struggle for India's Independence.* Minneapolis: Lerner Publications Co., 1982.

Index

125

Other Titles in the Lerner Biographies Series

About the Author

Carol Dommermuth-Costa has worked in the classroom as a teacher and in publishing as an editor. She now teaches creative writing for adults. Ms. Dommermuth-Costa has also published *Nikola Tesla: A Spark of Genius, Agatha Christie: Writer of Mystery, Emily Dickinson: Singular Poet,* and *William Shakespeare.* She lives in Mamaroneck, New York.

Photo Acknowledgments

The photographs are reproduced with the permission of: © Bettmann/ CORBIS, pp. 2, 71, 72; AP/ World Wide Photos, pp. 6, 82, 84, 88, 91, 93, 96, 101, 105, 111, 112, 114; © E.O. Hoppe/CORBIS, p. 9; ©Hulton Getty Picture Library/Archive Photos, p. 12, 40; © Hulton Getty Picture Library/Keystone/ Archive Photos, pp. 14, 16, 65, 110; Popperfoto/Archive Photos, pp. 19, 45, 74; © DPA/MKG/The Image Works, pp. 18, 33; © Topham/The Image Works, pp. 22, 48, 56, 64, 66, 78, 94, 108; © DPA/Images of India, pp. 24, 30, 36; Archive Photos, pp. 26, 51, 86, 98, 102;© Hulton-Getty/General Photographic Agency/Archive Photos, p. 42; Brown Brothers, p. 52; © Hulton-Deutsch Collection/CORBIS, p. 58; ©Max Desfor/AP Wide World Photos, p.61; © UPI/CORBIS/Bettmann, pp. 76, 90, 106, 115.

Cover: © Bettmann/CORBIS
Map illustrations by Tim Seeley